SALMON ON A DRY FLY

DEREK KNOWLES

Salmon on a Dry Fly

ILLUSTRATED WITH 14 COLOUR PLATES

H. F. & G. WITHERBY LTD.

First published in 1987 by
H. F. & G. WITHERBY LTD.
14 Henrietta Street,
London WC2E 8QJ

Filmset in Monophoto 13pt Apollo
and printed in Great Britain by
BAS Printers Limited,
Over Wallop, Hampshire

Foreword

by Rob Wilson

It has been my privilege to have known Derek Knowles since the late 60's and to have watched his efforts with his keeper, Albert Grant, to improve his river and develop it to its full potential. In this he displayed an analytical and contemplative attitude particularly to the problems of low water fishing.

Salmon anglers fall roughly into two categories, the traditionalists who work hard with revered rods, lines and flies and well kent techniques, and the innovators who are content to stick to old and ingrained methods so long as they work but who are prepared to experiment, to exercise the grey matter, and to develop techniques which pay off when for various accepted reasons fish are hopelessly off.

Derek, indubitably, falls into the second category and, happily for the rest of us, he has made notes of all the factors with a bearing on his successes when orthodoxy failed and the average salmon angler would have turned to golf. He has restated for us many of the lessons, well known to the average angler in terms of trout fishing but almost completely ignored where salmon are involved. Nor has he been motivated by avarice; on one occasion I had just taken a fish with him and he asked me if I wanted to keep it. On releasing the fish he calmly announced that it was the 34th to be put back that week! The important things to him are the hunt, the approach, the presentation and the hooking. He also takes great delight in defeating wily trout on the dap and the floater, and is a ghillie in the honours degree class!

I am sure that in this book your appetite will be whetted for a crack at the king of fish when other methods fail. Derek's floater technique is a challenge to us all and also a reminder that on many occasions we take great liberties with the sensitivities of what is a truly wild fish when fishing our more usual methods.

I am equally sure that it will be a landmark in the pursuit of piscatorial knowledge and will increase the potential for success at the more difficult end of the spectrum.

Brora, December 1986

9

Contents

List of Colour Plates

Acknowledgements

The writing of this book has given me tremendous pleasure and is based on a lifetime's fishing for everything from minnows to salmon. Knowledge is acquired from the writings of others, from fishing companions, friends, keepers, ghillies and odd acquaintances at the riverside. The constant exchange of information and experiences by all these people and the many chats and discussions which followed have all been sifted and tested and have had an influence on my thinking and experiments.

Many people have had a direct influence on the production of this book.

Mr Hugh Falkus who quoted my letters in his book *Salmon Fishing* and thereby sowed the literary seeds.

Mr Richard Atkinson of Cumbria whose enthusiastic response to my first efforts spurred me on.

Mr Albert Grant and Mr David Hudson of Sutherland who helped me in a very practical way with fishing experiments and many of the photographs in this book.

Mr Rob Wilson of Brora who had great faith in the Yellow Dolly concept and was kind enough to write the foreword for this book.

Mr Steven Wilson of New Brunswick who acted as my guide and gave me an insight into Canadian salmon fishing. Mr Jerry Doak of New Brunswick who allowed me to quote from his fishing catalogue.

Mr Antony Witherby who reviewed my efforts and gave me the benefit of his vast experience and then produced this book.

I am very grateful and thank them all for their help.

D.K.

1

Dry Fly Fishing for Salmon

Dry fly fishing is the most spectacular way of catching salmon, yet the least practised.

It is a way of fishing for all fishermen, expert, holiday fisherman or novice alike. If there are fish in the river, it is possible to catch them. The holiday angler tied to a particular week or fortnight, has only a 1 in 10 chance of finding the river in perfect order at the best of times. To such fishermen, dry fly fishing for salmon offers a ray of hope. When the river is showing its bones, all is not lost. The experts may moan about the lack of water, but it is far more important to have fish in the pools, even if they are potted and red. If they are not in the pools, even the expert will have a blank week.

Why is dry fly fishing for salmon not practised by the majority of fishermen? Is it that most of the books written on salmon fishing ignore 'dry fly' or dismiss it with a couple of paragraphs mentioning the failure of La Branche to catch the Scottish salmon. Most of the modern writers slide by the subject and content themselves with a mention of 'dibbling'. Some even promise more details in their future writings, when they have done a little more research.

The salmon fisherman is left with the distinct impression that dry fly is rather a waste of time, and the conventional way of sub-surface greased line fishing is really the only way to give any hope of success. In summer, when the river is in good order after a spate, the conventional way catches fish and catches them successfully. When the water falls, days of endless flogging follow. 'You should have been here last week (or month)' says the ghillie, as he yawns his way to the next spate. The experts write about the perfect conditions and follow on with glowing accounts of the odd fish caught by all manner of methods—even hammering away at him from dawn until dusk, in the hope that he will seize the fly like some irate neighbour seizing a ball that's been bounced endlessly at his fence.

Another possible reason for 'Dry Fly' to be ignored as a method for catching salmon, is that it promptly conjures up trout fishing, and the life-like imitations of natural flies that are taken for the real thing. Most fishermen know that salmon do not feed in fresh water, and that salmon flies are not flies, but brightly coloured lures. The word 'Fly' in salmon fishing parlance, means a feather and hair creation tied on hook or tube that is really a lure. A lure which, if it's the right size, threatens a salmon's territory, and is seized by him in an act of aggression. The conventional way of fishing for salmon is by fishing a 'fly' on a sunken line in Spring, to get the fly down to the fish, or just under the surface in summer.

Even when they have been used dry flies were based on imitations of natural flies, similar to trout fishing. Salmon have been caught on a dry fly when deliberately fished for, or by accident when trout fishing, but never in a consistent manner.

Many fishermen have tried dry fly for salmon without much success. One notable exception was Dr. Begg, who lived at Redesmouth on the North Tyne in Northumberland. In 1867 he was reputed to have caught over 150 salmon, mainly by dibbling a big hairy fly on a very short line. Incidentally, I caught my first dry fly Tyne fish on the water he used to fish just over 100 years before me. In spite of Dr. Begg's achievements, and those of Col. Frazer in 1922, who wrote about his experiments on the Test, dry fly was never accepted as a practical way of catching salmon.

The death knell to any real experiments came when George

La Branche failed to catch fish in the Dee in 1925.

George La Branche, along with two other Americans, Ambrose Monell and Edward Hewitt, developed a technique of dry fly fishing which was very successful in Canada.

Ambrose Monell was the creator, and he initiated his two friends in the art of dry fly fishing for salmon. The three of them developed a technique, and created dry flies which gave them some fantastic days of fishing for Atlantic Salmon in New Brunswick on the Eastern seaboard of Canada.

Hewitt wrote a book called *A Trout and Salmon Fisherman for Seventy-Five years* (1948) which I now consider to be the best book on fishing I have ever read. He had an enquiring mind, and puzzled away at all the problems connected with trout and salmon fishing, and his book, which covers all this in his experiences of 75 years of fishing, is well worth reading.

La Branche wrote *The Salmon and the Dry Fly* (1924), and describes in his book how he caught 23 salmon and grilse before lunch all on dry fly. These two books generated a lot of interest on this side of the Atlantic, and A. H. E. Wood was moved to invite La Branche to Cairnton on the Dee to demonstrate his method.

Arthur Wood was no slouch at salmon fishing, and his method of greased line fishing is used by all salmon fishermen to this day. The technique and flies used by Hewitt and La Branche were developed from their experiences as trout fishermen. It was from their training on brown trout that they developed their skill in catching salmon in low water conditions.

The dry fly which they perfected is shown in a coloured illustration with others in La Branche's book. It is the size and style of a Dapping May Fly. It looks like a size 8 long shank with a heavily palmered body, of the type used here and in Ireland for brown and sea trout fishing. My tying of this Colonel Monell fly is shown on plate 14 facing page 97.

They varied it only by going larger in size, and some of their flies were as much as two inches in diameter, as large as the biggest cock saddle hackles they could find.

La Branche in his book, recalls one day spent fishing with his friend, Col. Monell, on a very swift stretch of river. The Colonel fished the run down three times, each time with a different size of wet fly, before pronouncing that he could not make a fish move.

La Branche then fished the run with a dry fly working his way upstream. This way he didn't show himself to the fish or disturb the fish above him when playing a fish. When he got to the top of the run, he had caught four salmon, showing that there are occasions when a dry fly can succeed when other methods fail.

From their accounts of fishing the Restigouche River in New Brunswick, it is obvious that the waters were exceptionally clear. The fishermen and guides used to go downstream in a canoe and count the fish in the pools and note where they were lying, and then go back and fish for them.

La Branche often sent his guide up a suitable tree to spot the fish and give a commentary on the casting of the fly in relation to the fish, and give directions on where to cast to cover a particular fish.

In the summer of 1925, soon after the publication of his book, La Branche accepted the invitation to fish at Cairnton on the Aberdeenshire Dee, extended to him by Arthur Wood. When La Branche saw the Dee he was delighted. It was crystal clear, and so very like the Canadian rivers he fished at home. He was fairly certain in his own mind that he would be successful. He could count on his host, who knew the river intimately, to show him all the pools and lies that held fish. News of the demonstration travelled rapidly, and La Branche was accompanied by a gathering of fishermen who were keen to seen him display his skill. I have every sympathy for him, going on to a strange river with every move watched and scrutinised by so many capable fishermen.

He set about his task and many salmon rose to his fly, but not one took his hook, and success avoided him.

In his own words, 'Half a dozen fish came at the fly with wide open jaws, but even after taking it, did not close down on it'. This led to a theory developed between Wood and La Branche, that the fish had dislocated jaws and could not close them properly. I rather think that Wood was being a bit impish. Wood went further, and suggested quite forcibly, that in his opinion the strong hackle was stopping the hook from taking hold. He had seen at least 20 salmon take the fly down in such a manner that if he had been using one of his low water flies, the fish would have been hooked. This was all so disheartening for La Branche after travelling so far, and knowing that he could catch fish this way in Canada, but in four years at Cairnton, he killed only one salmon on dry fly.

So despite the success achieved by La Branche and Hewitt on the eastern seaboard of Canada, their method was not successful on this side of the Atlantic. The myth that salmon would not take a dry fly on this side of the Atlantic was created and extolled by the pundits, and that dry fly fishing for salmon was rather a waste of time.

Odd fish were caught by trout anglers, but no-one made any attempt to try dry fly in any serious way. Many reasons were given why dry fly did not work, and one persisted that, because the season in Canada was later, and the water warmer, salmon would not take a floating fly unless the water temperature was 70°. This was the way it remained until a few years ago when I went for a week's sea trout fishing on the Border Esk, organised by Hugh Falkus.

I was sitting by the river one night about 1.00 a.m. It was a nice soft summer's night, I had stopped fishing and was just enjoying the night, when Hugh came along to see how things were going. He sat down and we chattered for a while about fish-

ing in general, which led on to his forthcoming book on Salmon
Fishing. I asked if it would include anything about dry fly for
salmon. 'No', he said. 'That's a pity', said I, 'there have only been
two books written on dry fly as far as I know, by a couple of
Americans named Hewitt and La Branche, who caught salmon
in Canada, but could not catch them in Scotland. Whereas I've
found that it works like a charm, and I catch 60% of my salmon
on dry fly'. At this provocative statement, Hugh became quite
interested, and I gave him a rough description of my method.
He then suggested I should write about it in the form of a letter,
and this could be the way to include it in his book, which he
intended to be a very practical work on salmon fishing. I wrote
two or three letters to him, and they formed the basis for his chapter on Dry Fly Fishing. When the book was published, the 'Yellow
Dolly' went public and caused quite a stir.

The Christmas following the publication, I sat down and for
the first time read the chapter in his book very carefully. (I had
skimmed through it when it first came out without really reading
it). I then realised that I'd dangled the 'Yellow Dolly' in a very
tantalising way in front of the many salmon fishermen who would
read Hugh's book. This was borne out by the numerous people
who were suddenly interested in, and asking for, Yellow Dollies.
As it was impossible to give flies to everyone who asked for them,
I took a series of photographs showing an actual Yellow Dolly
in each stage of its construction.

I soon realized that possibly a fly by itself without some details
of how it should be fished was not an adequate answer, and from
there it was a short step for me to consider writing my own book
on the subject. I had spent some twelve years creating and
experimenting with the Yellow Dolly and in a book could convey
my experience, which might make a better starting point for any
fisherman attempting to catch a salmon on a dry fly. I was also
convinced the method could add to the enjoyment of the sport and

benefit in particular the holiday angler, unable to select his week's fishing, giving him an entertaining alternative to try out, when confronted with a week of drought conditions.

2

Creating the Fly

Fortunately, I had not read either Hewitt or La Branche until after I had created and made successful my method of dry fly fishing for salmon. If I had, I might never have succeeded. I would have been preconditioned to using big fuzzy flies and floating them without drag, in the same way as a trout fisherman. However, it was very interesting to read about the experiences of Hewitt and La Branche, and also of A. H. E. Wood and his method of greased line fishing.

All of us started from a very similar observation of fish behaviour, and the reaction of a salmon to a floating object. The Americans had their interpretation of the fishes behaviour and came up with their method, which I've already discussed.

A. H. E. Wood interpreted it in a completely different way, and devised his famous greased line method, using sparsely dressed low water flies just under the surface. Wood's description of sitting on a bridge dangling a fly is fascinating to me, because it mirrored my own experience, but my interpretation was very different to his.

My experience and experiment was in Ireland on a little sea trout river that had a small run of salmon in June and July. It was a short length of river from the sea to a chain of lochs which offered some first class fishing. This short stretch had been improved with numerous caulds and weirs to make holding pools. The river was very low at the particular time I am writing about. In fact, it was always low whenever I went. The locals were always saying 'You should have been here last week, etc. etc.'.

20

There is one weir where the river is channelled into an 8 foot width by stone walls, with a little wooden footbridge for crossing from one bank to the other. I was sitting on this bridge one day, watching the stream emerging from the restriction of the walls, and spreading into the pool below.

I saw a salmon flash just on the edge of the current where it eddied behind the wall. I kept watching and saw it flash again. I had with me, not a fly rod, but a 16 foot dapping pole. I had spent the early morning stalking one of the pools, hopefully not showing myself, blow lining a grasshopper over the bank on to the water for a sea trout. Seeing this salmon flashing restlessly in the water, I tied on an artificial winged Mayfly, poked out the pole, and bounced the Mayfly on top of the water. Splash! the fish lunged at it, but did not take it. I tried again, splash! the fish still did not take it, and then would not come again, even though I bounced the fly in a most tantalising way. I sat for ten minutes and then tried again. This time, just as the fly touched down, the wind caught the fly and it skated along the surface. Splash, the fish had it, and I had a very spirited struggle with a fresh fish on an extremely sloppy rod. Most interesting, the fly stationary and he splashed at it—skidding along the water, and he took it. Into the memory file it went.

The following year I was fishing a little higher up the river, where there's a cauld which in low water channels the river into a narrow stream that feeds the head of the next pool. It is about 20 feet wide with long grass and rushes lining the banks. The water was about three feet deep with a nice flow. I again saw a fish flash, this time in the middle of the stream. He was restless. Every few minutes he would roll and twist in the water causing his side to flash briefly and it was this that gave his position away. I was fishing with a little Badger Tube Fly and I cast this for the fish upstream first, and made nothing of him. I then backed off and went around and fished downstream, and still couldn't make

anything of him. He had not taken any notice of the fly and was
not aware of my presence and continued to roll and twist. I crept
away, sat down, scratched my head, and decided to try and dibble
him. I tied a loop in the leader, cut one end and tied on a slightly
larger black stoat's tail on an Esmond Drury hook. Crawling this
time I got into position by the run, sheltered I hoped by a clump
of grass. I cast the flies on a short line to the far side of the run
slightly upstream of the fish, and by using the Badger Tube as
a drag anchor, slowly brought the Stoat's tail across the stream.
The fly was just dragging on the surface and as it came over the
fish it promptly came up and took it. More information for the
memory file.

Dibbling is a style of fishing practised on the Helmsdale in the
north of Scotland and on other northern rivers. It consists of a
tail fly used as a drag to hold the leader, so that the bob fly can
be worked bouncing across the current. It is fished on a very
short line, where the current comes close into the bank. It is quite
an exciting way of fishing, because you see the fish come at the
fly. It is very effective, particularly where the water is fairly
rough.

I think it works well in rough water because the fish cannot
see the fisherman standing there like some great heron. Dr. Begg,
as mentioned, practised this form of fishing in the 1860's. The
fly he used is described as rabbit fur for the body and large tufts
for wings. This would make a fly similar in appearance to the
Wulff series of flies and could be bounced or skittered in the
manner of dibbling or fished on the surface with drag.

I was greatly intrigued by dibbling, but it had by my standards
very limited application due to the very short line used to bring
the dropper along the surface even in rough water. I had caught
a lot of fish with a $1\frac{1}{2}''$ aluminium tube dibbled across the runs
when the river was high and falling after a spate, but again it
was at short range. At the back of my mind was the need for

a way of dibbling at a greater distance, and utilising the full casting ability of the rod.

One day tying up some small Badger Tube Flies on thin copper cored electric cable, I decided to try and make the hair stand out on a couple of them, to see whether this would make the tips of the hair vibrate more attractively than the normal flat tying. Fishing with them, I found that they had a tendency to stay on top of the water until they got into broken water, and then they went under. I greased them to see if this would help to keep them on top of the water and fish with a wake like a dibbled fly, and I caught a fish. The first step had been taken unknowingly, I was still thinking about dibbling and trying to fish at a greater distance. I tied many tubes, but still had a problem with them drowning in the broken water. Puzzling away at the problem, and thinking of how I could get better floatation, I decided to duplicate the flare of hair, and tied it on the head of the tube. This I hoped would make it lay on the water, and hold up the head. Just by chance, I picked up a Fallow Deer Tail that I'd recently dyed yellow for hair to make 2" Garry Dogs to use when the river was in spate. Tying the yellow hair on to the red tube, I used the black from the fallow tail for the other end. I varnished the whipping on the black end, and pulled out the copper wire, stood it up on its yellow skirt to dry. There looking at me, standing an inch tall, was a little doll with a yellow skirt, a red bodice, a black shawl and a black face. I named it there and then 'Yellow Dolly'. On plate 3 is shown one of my first tyings.

I fished with it, and it moved a lot of fish, which was very exciting, because they threw themselves at it in a most aggressive manner. But the only fish it actually caught was after it had sunk in the rough water!

However, I persisted, and because I had not read about the American way of dry fly fishing, I went smaller to three-quarters of an inch and caught a few fish, and had many exciting moments seeing the fish come to the fly. I have always operated on the principle that if a fish moves at your fly, whether trout or salmon, go smaller, because I think the fish is nervous of the size. I continued off and on with experiments, tying single skirts and threading them on the nylon to give different shapes, and putting three or four on together. The trend was to a smaller and smaller fly with the accompanying problem of treble hooks being too heavy for the fly, and sinking it, and the worry that anything less than size 12 was far too small for a salmon.

However, with the smaller flies, smaller trebles had to be used or the fly sank. I used a combination of grease on the fly, then on the hook, then on the leader, which also got thinner. I caught more fish and gained confidence in the holding power of size 16 and 18 trebles. I even went down to size 20, but found that they were just too light. I caught a small grilse, about 5 lbs, on a size 20 treble. He was on one hook which was all but straightened, and I was very lucky to land him. What was developing through all this experimenting, *was the need to keep the fly right on top of the water.*

The salmon has extraordinarily good eye-sight. There's absolutely no doubt that the fish can see the fly a long way off. A small fly in rough water appears to the fisherman, if he can see it at all, to be such a tiny insignificant thing, that salmon would never look at it, but be assured the fish can see it, and it's a very significant thing to him.

I called at Pitlochry one day to have a look at their fish ladder and viewing chamber. Unfortunately, there were no fish there at the time, but I was fascinated watching the water flowing through the chamber with the back lighting of the chamber showing every detail. What appeared to be clean water was full of little bits of debris and bubbles, all swirling through. If a loose fly had been amongst the debris, it would have been another piece of debris amongst many. However, attach the fly to a length of

PLATE 1

The Author

PLATE 2

THE TYING OF A YELLOW DOLLY

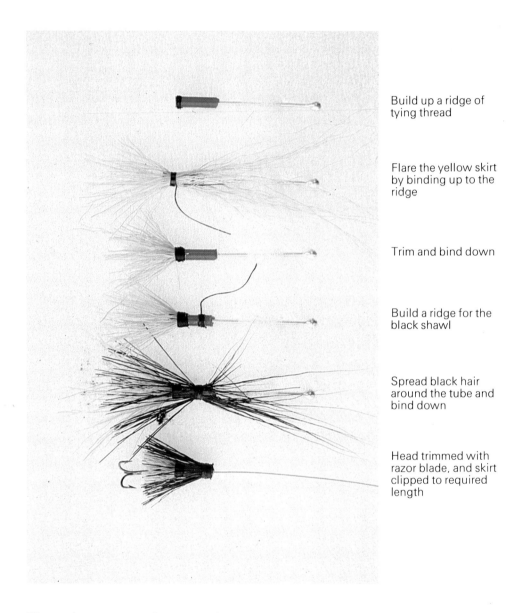

Build up a ridge of
tying thread

Flare the yellow skirt
by binding up to the
ridge

Trim and bind down

Build a ridge for the
black shawl

Spread black hair
around the tube and
bind down

Head trimmed with
razor blade, and skirt
clipped to required
length

The various stages of construction are
described on pages 28 and 29

PLATE 3

Yellow Dolly tied on copper-cored
electric cable

"Put this on"

Useful sizes, 54° and higher

Looking at me was a little doll

Enlarged Yellow Dolly

PLATE 4

The drag of the cast does not frighten
salmon

nylon, and its progress would be retarded, behaving differently to the patterns set up by all the other inert bits of matter. It would, by contrast, have independent movement, giving it life. I came away firmly convinced that to allow a fly to go with the current was impossible if attached to a nylon leader. Therefore, drag on a fly was always present, and was an aid and not a handicap. I've followed that principle since, even with trout on a dead calm day. When fishing dry fly on the loch, I move the fly, albeit very slowly, and I think I get more offers than leaving it perfectly stationary, the movement attracts without frightening. Encouraged by what I had seen at Pitlochry, I fished with more movement on the fly. The inch long fly I started experimenting with, became $\frac{3}{4}$ of an inch, and then smaller. The copper-cored electric cable was too thick for smaller flies, and a thinner piece of red plastic tube was used. A problem with plastic is the slipperiness of the surface. Super glue helped to hold the hair in place once I'd locked it in with thread. These little tiny flies $\frac{3}{8}''$ long, were just about as small as I could tie them with a shawl and skirt. They proved very successful at inducing fish to take, but despite their success, I thought that something even smaller was needed in my armoury.

I tied yellow badger hair on to a tiny length of tube. Doing this I wore surgeon's spectacles, which are a great aid when tying flies, particularly as I'm getting older — poor chap.

The result was a tiny fly just a quarter of an inch long overall, with a skirt of about a dozen hairs. That little fly I still have and use. Whenever I have moved a fish with the smallest Yellow Dolly, this little fly is the final weapon. If I can't make the salmon open its mouth for this tiny morsel, I give him best.

I've discussed the thinking that went into the creation of the 'Yellow Dolly', and the path that I followed, and how my method diverged from the paths of Wood and La Branche. It is very intriguing the way a simple observation made when sitting on a bridge over a stream developed — how the bits of information, observations, experiences and experiments came together and resulted in the Yellow Dolly.

Arthur Wood followed a path that led to slim sparsely dressed flies fished sub-surface and which is now recognised as greased line fishing.

George La Branche tied big fuzzy flies imitating natural flies which he floated on the surface without drag.

I produced a small light fly with a shape that floated on top of the water and kept it there when drag was induced by the current or by hand stripping in slack water.

The most striking thing to emerge from my experiments was the dramatic response of many salmon to a small object sliding across the surface. Not bouncing, dibbling or skittering but a nice steady draw brushing the surface all the time over wave and ripple.

Drag, abhorred by Wood and La Branche, actually created an aggressive response from the salmon. I do not hold up my style as better than the others. I just offer it as a different approach to making the salmon open his mouth. If he does not, you will not catch him.

So when all else fails, try a 'Yellow Dolly'.

3

Tying the Fly

The construction of the Yellow Dolly came about after much experimenting, and is so made that it will ride on top of the water. It will stay on the surface in most conditions, but can be drowned if it is drawn too quickly in rough water.

The essential thing for the making of the fly is strong springy hair, which means a coarse hair. When I first tied the fly, I was lucky to have the tail of a fallow deer which I had shot and then dyed while it was still fresh. This hair I've found to be the best I have ever used. It keeps its spring in spite of being greased, soaked and chewed by salmon. I have used frozen Fallow Tails, but they go soft when greased. This softening of the hair is a problem. If the hair goes soft, it doesn't retain the cone shape which keeps it on top of the water. Buck Tail appears to be the best alternative. I dye the hair with 'Dylon Sunglow No. 2' by simmering for 15 minutes then rinsing under the tap. Overcooking turns it an orange yellow. If a black and white tail is dyed then the black hair which does not change colour will make the shawl.

For the tube I use a piece of copper cored electric cable with an outside diameter of $\frac{3}{32}''$. It's a very useful size for making small tube flies, and very convenient for practising tying the larger Yellow Dollies. Clip off a one and a half inch length of cable or slightly longer. Run a cut round the middle of the cable with a razor blade or scalpel, and pull off one end of the insulating sheath.

The bared copper wire is ideal for holding the tube of cable in the fly tying vice.

If you refer to the colour photograph on plate 2 between pages

27

24 and 25 you will see the various stages of construction.

The first and most important part is to whip on a ridge of tying thread as near to one end as possible without the thread collapsing.

This ridge is built up by taking turns of thread round and round the same point. When the thread has been built up into a little ridge, similar to that shown in the photograph, take a little tuft of yellow hair clipped from the base of the deer tail, spread this around the tube as shown, with the thick end of the hair forming the skirt. Catch the hair in with two or three turns of thread, then spread the hair evenly round the tube, pulling out any surplus. Then starting a $\frac{1}{16}''$ from the ridge of thread, bind the hair down, winding towards the little ridge. As the thread nears the ridge, the hair will start to flare, keep binding down until the hair stands out an an angle of between 30 and 45 degrees. Nip off the strands of surplus hair lying along the tube with fine scissors, dab on a spot of varnish, and finish binding down with a couple of whip finishes. The finished length of the binding should be less than one eighth of an inch. Snip off the tying thread and allow to dry.

The tying of the black shawl is a repeat of the process used for the skirt. The positioning of the second collar of tying thread determines the finished length of fly.

For your first practise run, leave a gap of about $\frac{1}{4}''$ to show the colour of the red tube.

Build up the ridge of thread then take a pinch of black hair, catch it in with two or three turns of thread, evenly spread it around the tube, use very little hair, so that it doesn't hide the colour of the tube. The hair should extend beyond the length of the finished fly. Tie it down in the same manner as for the skirt.

Pull the fly off the copper wire while it is still clamped in the vice, clip the yellow and black hair to the required length. Both the black shawl and the yellow skirt have the same hem line. The head of the tube can be clipped to length with a sharp razor blade, which will remove the surplus sheath and hair. The finished result should be similar to the final stage shown in the photograph. A good shape and thickness of dressing is shown in the enlarged photograph on plate 3. For the smaller sizes I use a red plastic tube with an outside diameter of $\frac{1}{16}$ of an inch.

If you are lucky enough to get some very good hair which is coarse and springy, then half a dozen flies will last all season. the construction, done properly, gives an extremely hard wearing fly. However, you will find that once you can make them, friends and snags have a way of multiplying the numbers required very rapidly. I'm afraid my fly box has a few tatty remnants, no matter how many I tie I never have any decent ones.

I have been asked, 'Why red, yellow and black, why not other colour combinations? Blue Dollies, Black Dollies etc . . .' The answer is very simple. I had black and yellow hair and red tube, and I put them together and they caught a lot of fish. I have never had a feeling or a need to tie any other colours. In fact, I don't think colour has any real contribution to make to the fly, except that the yellow of the skirt is more visible than any other colour, and this is a great help when fishing. I wouldn't fish with the same confidence if the Yellow Dolly didn't have a yellow skirt.

I have experimented to some extent with other colour combinations, and all-black dollies, but never fished seriously with them. I know they will catch fish. One day a friend of mine was fishing the river, and I went down around lunchtime to see how he was getting on. I found him full of despair, he had just been broken by a fish, and not only that, he had lost his 'Yellow Dolly'. 'Could I let him have another'? he asked. I rummaged in my plastic box, I only had two and they were on the small side, but there was a very nice all-black one, about $\frac{5}{8}$ of an inch long. 'Try this', I said. His face dropped at the sight of the black fly, but he took it and I left him to his fishing.

Late that afternoon, he came staggering into the fish larder, having carried a 12 lb. fish all the way up the river. He thinks 'Black Dollies' are nearly as good as yellow.

The yellow colour certainly helps to show the fly, and it is important to pick out the fly and follow its progress over the water. Then you can correct any tendency for the fly to drown and sink, or from the action of the fly, appreciate that the treble is hooked up in the head of the fly.

The hooking of a treble can be an occasional problem, if it occurs often, it is because either the nylon has a kinky bit above the eye of the hook caused when pulling up the knot, or the hook is too large for the dressing. A good indication that the treble is hooked in the head of the fly is when the fly sinks when it should fish properly in the type of water being fished.

The success of the fly is in its shape, which holds it on top of the water, and its lightness. Anything which detracts from this concept, is detrimental to its performance. Treble hooks should be small, light and strong, with short shanks.

The hooks I use are mainly Mustad, they were the only ones I could get until recently. At one stage, I was down to only five size 18 trebles, and they were very precious. Three of them stayed in my fly-tying kit, I couldn't risk them all in the same box.

The use of little bits of rubber tube to keep the hook in line is the method favoured on ordinary tube flies. I have tried this with the Yellow Dolly but it adds weight to the fly, and impairs its ability to stay on top of the water. I rely on the skirt and the treble being matched. I do lose the odd fish, due to the treble catching in the top of the tube, but because the fly is so light, it creates a lot more opportunities, and on balance, catches far more fish.

4

Fishing the Yellow Dolly

Having tied or acquired an armoury of Yellow Dollies in sizes $\frac{5}{8}''$, $\frac{1}{2}''$ and $\frac{3}{8}''$, all that's needed now is the technique to make the most of them. Fishing the fly is easy for any dry fly trout fisherman, and not difficult for others less experienced, if I can convey the instructions in an understandable way. The chances of which are remote indeed. When I was 14, I sat the end of term exams, and in French, English and Latin; I was 34th out of 37 in all three subjects. The consistency made me think the other 3 students were absent.

The equipment needed consists of Rod, Line, Nylon, Scissors, Grease, Flies, Treble Hooks, and a priest.

I shall go through all the items in detail, and explain the whys and wherefores, and also describe what I use.

The rod should preferably be single-handed 9 or 10 feet long, fitted with a good quality line.

A single handed rod is so much easier to fish with when the water is low and the salmon need to be stalked.

Summer fishing is the time for small flies, dry or wet, and floating lines which transform rod fishing into a delight far removed from the drudgery of sinking lines and the long rods of spring fishing.

In summer, with the higher temperatures, fish run well and the best of the fishing is further up river than in spring. In the tributaries and upper reaches of the main river the pools are not so big, and casts of great length are no longer the norm.

Therefore I strongly recommend a 9 ft or 10 ft rod. The latter is possibly the best length for the average fisherman if he has a reasonably strong wrist. With a rating of AFTM 7–8 a ten foot rod will cast an AFTM No. 7 line with great ease. The line can be either a double taper floater, which is the better shape of line for switch casts and roll casts, and shoots nicely through the rod rings, or a weight forward floater which is not so good for roll casts or switch casts but will shoot line two or three yards further. On balance the double taper is the better choice as it has the added advantage that both ends can be used and reversed when the line end gets worn, and this doubles the line's life.

I use a nine foot carbon fibre rod rated AFTM 6–7 fitted with a white weight forward No. 7 floating line. With it I can cast and shoot a reasonable length of line without false casting. It is a comfortable rod to use and I can fish all day without any wrist strain. It is also very much easier to stalk a fish with a single handed rod than a double handed fourteen footer. The low rating of my rod allows me to use 6–8 lbs nylon without any risk of breaking when I lift the rod to tighten in to a fish. The reel should be fitted with at least a hundred yards of backing just in case the fish takes off and attempts to go to sea. It also aids the recovery of the fly line by filling the reel to full capacity.

Grease—I use Mucilin, none of the liquids or sprays I have used give as good a performance, or are as long lasting.

Flies as I've described, and treble hooks in sizes 16 and 18, light short-shanked and sharp.

A priest is quicker than searching for a suitable weapon, and therefore less cruel.

This then is the ideal outfit and very similar to that for trout with the exception of the flies and trebles. Indeed I use my rods for trout fishing on the rivers and lochs as well as for salmon fishing.

If, where you are going to fish, requires casting more distance than can be comfortably done with a 10 foot rod, then a light

PLATE 5

Concealment is all important. The Author casting downstream

Drawing the fly across the current

PLATE 6

Side strain makes the fish work

Michael Joicey playing a fish at the 'Rock Pool'

double-handed rod in carbon will give the additional distance. I have a 14 foot rod rated 9–10, which has a nice easy action, which I use on the big flat pools where I need to stand well back from the water to avoid frightening the fish.

Using a double-handed rod with 8 lbs. nylon requires a lighter setting on the reel than for normal salmon fishing, otherwise it's easy to be broken by a strong fish that takes line quicker than the reel gives it. I have been broken a couple of times because I had neglected to lighten the reel setting when using 8 lbs. nylon.

Now, imagine that you are by the riverside with your single-handed rod, its white floating line, ten feet of 8 lb. nylon leader, and a $\frac{5}{8}''$ Yellow Dolly, with a size 16 treble. The fly, hook, cast and the first yard of the fly line should be greased with Mucilin. If you know the river, then you will know which pools and runs hold fish, and where the fish are lying. I will describe a typical pool, and the way I would advise an angler to approach it.

Let us assume that the fishing has been good, but the river is getting low, and fishing the conventional fly is only producing the odd fish. Now is the ideal time to try something else, like dry fly.

The imaginary pool we are going to fish will give me a chance to make a few points as we fish it down.

It has a nice bit of rough at the head which spreads into the pool with one or two lies in the current, where it slows and deepens into the pool.

The first thing to do before going anywhere near the river's edge is to survey the pool from a distance. You may have fished the pool many times before, and there is a well-worn path made by anglers fishing their way down the pool, but keep well away.

The first taking lie is about 15 yards out from the bank, where the rough enters the pool. It's a well known place and you may have caught one or two fish there on other occasions.

As we stand looking at the pool, I make this point to you. If only the odd fish are now being caught, is it possible that in the lower water conditions the fish are being frightened by the presence of the fisherman? Salmon, when they are aware of fishermen, settle slightly in the water, and when so alerted, are no longer taking fish. Also if the fish have been flogged over in low water they will become as wild as hawks and bolt down the pool at the slightest movement to fling themselves out of the water some 30 yards downstream.

The vast majority of salmon fisherman appear to be completely unaware that they themselves are responsible for fish being impossible to catch in low water. No wild creature will remain undisturbed by the nearness of a human being and salmon are wild creatures. The fisherman should be very very wary in his approach if he wants to catch a salmon in low water.

The first thing to decide is the best and least obtrusive spot from where you can comfortably cast a fly to cover the lie, also the three or four yards of rough water above the lie that could hold a fish.

Having decided the spot to cast from, we could walk over to the edge of the river and cast at the lie. That sort of approach, used by many fishermen, would skyline us, as there is very little cover, and no background. A better approach would be to crouch, going forward and then crawl the last 5 or 6 yards, and sit a yard or two back from the edge of the bank. Having done that, we are now sitting comfortably, and as no fish have suddenly hurled themselves out of the water and all remains quiet we can assume that we have not been seen. There is no hurry. When you are ready draw a couple of yards of fly line out of the top ring and flick the fly on to the water. See the fly floats, and then creates a little wake as the current pulls at it. Pull another length of line off the reel with your left hand (if you are right-handed), keep the line that goes up the rod trapped under your right index finger.

Lift the rod to draw the fly, and then lift the index finger to let the loose line be drawn up the rod at the start of the back cast.

The cast should be made square across the river.

Follow the fly with the point of the rod as it fishes round, and draw another pull of line from the reel. A pull of about two feet draws some three feet of line off the reel if the line is trapped under the forefinger of the casting hand. Cast again, and you should feel a slight weight in the line, and the fly will land some twenty feet away, and near to the edge of the rough. The next cast will be just into the rough, but still well clear of the lie. The fly can be seen riding along the water very nicely.

Lift the rod as the fly comes round to keep the fly moving and draw more line, keeping the line trapped under the index finger. Accelerate the lift of the rod into the back cast without easing the pressure of the index finger and as the line goes out on the forward cast ease the pressure off the fore finger, and the weight of the line going forward will draw out the loop of line, shooting it the extra three feet. This is the way to make each cast shoot the extra line and fish through a three foot greater arc with each cast.

What we want to avoid is false casting, which is an abomination, frightening fish, wasting effort and completely unnecessary.

Once the weight of line is available to shoot the extra line, strip line in over index finger of the rod hand to keep the fly moving as it comes out of the flow into the slower water. By lifting the rod slowly at the end of the stripping, the fly can be moved another few feet, and the transition into the cast is done without any jerk or snatching the fly off the water. Fish often take as the fly starts to accelerate. Stripping is the term I use for pulling line over the index finger of my rod hand which also clamps the line to the rod handle when the other hand stops pulling line.

This stripping action puts movement on the fly particularly when fishing the long flat pools that have insufficient current to move the fly. The spare line that accumulates I either gather by looping every second pull in my hand to form yard long loops or drop them on the ground. Stripping is not to be confused with the finger twiddling figure of eight line recovery, it is long steady pulls of a yard or more at a time to keep the fly buzzing along the slacker water.

Hopefully, you are now into this nice easy style of fishing, sitting quietly on the bank. Each cast covering more water and casting a little bit more downstream than square across as the line lengthens. Judge this by the pace of the stream and the behaviour of the fly. Mend the line if necessary, but keep the fly moving across the water like a swimming sedge or a tiny speedboat.

Forget everything you have ever read about drag on a fly frightening salmon, it doesn't, it attracts them when the fly is on the surface.

If the fly goes under crossing the rough water, ease the pull on the fly, and the air bubble trapped by the skirt as it sinks will bob it back onto the surface.

The next cast you make is going to bring the fly over the lie. The fly lands 2 or 3 yards upstream of the lie, the flow of the water carries it down stream and the pull of the line brings it over the lie just upstream of the break on the surface. Nothing! The fly comes a couple of yards past the lie, and you start to draw (strip) line. A head suddenly comes out of the water, and a big silver body slides right past the fly. You struck as if you had been shot! No harm done. The fish didn't take the fly, and he was past before you snatched it away. Better strip in the line to look at the fly and see that everything is OK. Don't wind any line on to the reel, you have the right length of line to recast for the fish lying on the ground. You also have a fish that's interested in your Yellow Dolly, and providing you don't do anything stupid to frighten it, you have a very good chance of catching him.

Right, if you've calmed down and your heart attack is over, make a couple of false casts downstream away from the holding part of the river to lengthen the line, then cast a couple of yards short of the lie. Don't, for goodness sake, work out line by false casting over the fish. Good, now cover the lie, Nothing! He didn't even follow the fly. Try him again, Nothing! Strip in your line. There's no point in a third cast. Look at your flies and select one an $\frac{1}{8}''$ shorter, the same treble should do. Grease everything up again, and this time, fish the smaller fly in the same arcs as the first time down so that all the water is fished down to the lie.

There could be other fish in the rough water above the lie, and the change in size may attract them.

That's nice, keep the fly moving across the rough water, another three casts and you should cover the fish.

Splash! A fish has taken your fly; lift your rod, keep hold of the line with your forefinger, feel the weight of him, don't strike: The hook sets itself when you feel the fish. Look at your reel to see the line is clear. Stand up, let him have the line, but keep a steady pressure on him. Wind up the reel. Good, you have him on the reel. Now it is up to you.

A good tip for getting slack line on to the reel when a fish has taken, is to play the fish with the forefinger regulating the pressure on the line by trapping it against the rod, while the line that comes on to the reel is passed between the little and third finger of the same hand. This way the reel can be wound up to take the slack without any kinks or loops going onto the reel, and if the fish runs towards you the line can be stripped through the finger to keep in contact with the fish.

You were keen to catch a fish on a dry fly, so you must have caught and played salmon before, so I will let you play it, but remember, we did not bring a net.

You haven't tailed a fish before. Good! It's time you did. Nets are such an awful nuisance to carry around. They get left behind, trip you up, catch on buttons, briars etc., and quite often have been left at the previous pool when you hook a fish.

What you must do, is look for a suitable place to beach him, and on this pool, it's going to be easy. There's a nice shingle beach just below you. The first thing you must do, however, is tire him out, and that is done very simply by making him work. Do not let him rest; keep him moving. When you first hook him, you play him with a high rod to keep the line out of the water and avoid getting hung up on rocks and other snags, drop the rod when the fish jumps to slacken the line, just in case he lands on it. The first few runs of a fish can be quite dramatic as he tears line off the reel. Make no attempt to check him. Let the reel sing but be ready to recover line as soon as the reel stops. When he stops, you may feel a tug tug action like a terrier shaking a rat. It is a bit unnerving but keep cool the fish is thrashing his body from side to side in great arcs and snapping his jaws. Just hope he will do more of it, this behaviour tires a fish more quickly than any other.

When the frantic runs are over, and you feel the fish tiring, and he tries to lay in the water, don't lift him with a high rod, but pull him sideways with side pressure. This moves his head across the current, and the current moves him towards you. He will keep swimming to regain his balance in the flow, and you keep pulling him off balance. This also is very tiring for the fish, particularly if you can get him to do steady surging pulls into the current.

When he rolls over and shows his flank, you've nearly got him, but keep at him, he still has some energy left. When he rolls over a few more times, bring him slowly towards the beach. When he feels the gravel, he'll make back into the deep with a little frantic surge. Let him have line, but keep up the steady pull and he will soon come back to the beach. As he grounds on the gravel do not try to pull him up the beach. Just hold him and he will flop onto his side. Strip line through your finger to keep a steady pressure on him, and walk to his tail. Do not pull the fly line through the top ring. Now, bend down and grasp him round the tail. If he's a salmon, pick him up, or push him up the beach. Don't worry which way your hand should be or think of using a handkerchief, or anything like that. What comes naturally is the right way to tail a fish. Your thumb and first finger grip the fish round the small of the tail. If it's a small fish, 7 lbs. or less, depending on the river, it is most likely a grilse, and they don't have a bump on the tail to hold your grip. They can squirt out of your hand like a trout. So if it's a small fish, take more care and grip him firmly, with your thumb and finger nipping firmly into the flesh on the top and underside of the body just in front of the tail before picking him up or sweep him up the beach with the side of your foot.

After the first one, you'll throw away your net, and learn to deal with all the other situations you will be presented with.

When the fish has been safely landed, the first thing to do is hit him with the priest before taking the hook out, unless you are returning him to the river. The place to hit him is on top of the head just behind the eyes. If you look at the top of the salmon's head, you will see the scale marks on its body, end at a line where the head is smooth, hit him $\frac{1}{2}$ an inch in front of that line, and he'll only need one bonk.

The pool is now nicely disturbed after all the activity, but the fish you have caught wasn't the one that moved to the bigger fly. There is no-one else waiting to fish the pool so let us move quietly away from the pool and go downstream and have lunch at the tail of the pool.

Lunch is a grand time to recall the morning's sport, whether fishing or shooting.

Grand lunches are not for fishing days or shooting on the hill, they have to be carried. An orange and a chocolate biscuit is ample, allaying the pangs of hunger and giving a healthy appetite for supper.

Let us go over the morning's fishing while we eat. The main thing that should have come over, is the easy, possibly lazy approach to the business of catching a salmon.

The first survey of the pool to pinpoint and memorize the features. The careful concealed approach and the time taken to get comfortable, and make certain that everything is in order. The covering of the water in methodical sweeps to show the fly briefly to any fish that could be between you and the intended lie. The change of tactics when the fish would not take. Going smaller and fishing all the water again down to the lie, and the taking of a fish that was not the intended one. If we had done what a lot of fishermen would do. Change to a smaller fly and recast immediately for the fish that had moved, we may have caught it, but we would have missed the one we have in the bag, and the other is still to be fished for.

A salmon that is settled in a pool does not vacate his lie unless disturbed, and he will return to it fairly quickly. So we can be fairly certain that our fish is back in his lie.

Never flog on for a fish after he's risen and not taken the fly. He didn't take it because he didn't want to.

I know people preach that you cannot over-fish a lie, but that attitude shows a complete lack of understanding of the natural order of things. He's not going to run away, and we will achieve a lot more with stealthy unobtrusiveness.

Finished lunch? Right! Change your leader for a new one, and regrease, you are going to fish for this salmon as though he's a big brown trout, and fish upstream as you would for trout with a dry fly. There are two lies in the middle of the pool below the one we know holds our fish. You will be fishing over those two first so we must get into position below the lowest lie without disturbing any fish.

A little detour away from the pool and then a slow crouching approach, a final crawl and then you can kneel a few yards from the edge of the water. Cast 30° upstream, and when you've got enough line out and can shoot 4 or 5 yards more you should be covering water 15 or 16 yds upstream. Move upstream by walking on your knees or shuffling on your backside between casts. You will fish over the two lies in the middle of the pool, and then the one you know holds a fish.

That's fine, strip line in so that the fly travels a little faster than the current, keep the rod low so that when you stop stripping you can keep the fly moving by lifting the rod, and then easily into the back cast.

Fine! You have passed over the first lie, and seen nothing. Keep on fishing. Grand! That's over the second lie, Plosh! Plosh! A fish came out of the water on the far side, either the fly or the line frightened him out of that lie. I know you didn't see him leave, but the way he came out of the water, I'm quite certain he was a frightened fish. Keep on fishing. You will have to strip a bit faster as the current gets stronger, and cast a little more upstream.

Now as you come up to the lie with the fish in, try and cover it by getting the fly upstream of the lie, and the line just on the boil.

See his neb come out? He rose at the fly. Try him again, there he's up again. Well done! You didn't try to strike, Try him again. Oh dear! He's not having any. Strip in, you must go smaller. That little one $\frac{3}{8}$ inch long, and use a size 18 treble. Grease everything—Good—but wait five minutes for the sun to go back behind the clouds, and you will give yourself a better chance. The salmon sees too much when the sun shines.

Right! Work up to the fish again. That's fine! Next cast. Good!

Beautifully placed. Crikey! See his open jaws. He roared at it, and he's taken it. You've got him.

Believe me or not, as you wish, but that's a fair description of what can happen when you fish with a dry fly for salmon, upstream or down, and the success that can be achieved.

I shall now pick out one or two points, and deal with them in a little more detail.

The use of a single-handed rod is for ease of use, and accuracy of casting, and is ample to account for any normal summer fish. Some fishermen have the idea that salmon fishing requires double-handed rods sixteen feet long to deal with the mighty salmon. In fact, such rods are ideal for casting 3" flies, and lifting sinking lines and really belong to spring fishing and springers.

They do serve a purpose during summer spates, when 2" flies are needed. It's very difficult to cast a 2" Brass Tube with a 9 foot rod. It does a loop-the-loop, and either whistles past your ear or your ankle, and can be very dangerous in a wind. I know many salmon fishermen are purists who only fish for salmon regarding trout as vermin to be eliminated from the streams and burns so that the fry and parr have less competition. They insist on long rods for all salmon fishing spring and summer, large rivers and small. They get tremendous pleasure out of their rods but I do think they miss out on the additional skills that give added pleasure to the more versatile fisherman. I believe that the trout fisherman who fishes for salmon is a more skilled fisherman than the salmon fisherman who does not fish for trout.

To really get the maximum enjoyment out of Yellow Dolly fishing, use a single-handed rod. A double taper line is a beautiful line to fish with, easy to mend and roll to keep in contact with the fly.

The weight forward line allows more water to be fished, and makes shooting line so much easier, and because the flies are small, it turns the leader over very nicely. I use a weight forward line because it suits my style of fishing. I cannot fish without stripping line, a habit I have acquired over the years, expensive on lines but I think it catches me more fish. The white line shows on the water and helps your eye to pick up the fly, which can be very difficult to see in broken water, even with its yellow skirt.

A leader of level nylon with a breaking strain of 6 or 8 lbs. is ample to deal with the salmon, providing you lift the rod and do not strike as at a brownie. You will break in the fish if you do strike in the manner of a trout fisherman. A salmon in the water is a very unyielding object. It is very interesting that Hewitt, with his style of dry fly fishing, insisted that the diameter of the cast was very important, and used gut casts of .010 ins. with a B.S. of only 2 lbs. Modern nylon of the same diameter is 7 lbs. Hewitt could kill salmon on 2 lbs. B.S. gut leaders, albeit he used 600 yards of backing and a netsman (ghillie) to net his fish.

I use 6 lbs., and always change the leader after every fish. A leader only costs 10p, so there is no benefit in making a leader catch two fish, the chances of losing the second fish are too great. Experience is a good taskmaster. When spring fishing, I change the leader many times between fish and I use 25 lb. nylon, so I am not a light tackle fanatic. In summer, fine tackle gives a greater chance of success. I do not use tapered leaders when salmon fishing preferring to clip a length of leader from a spool of nylon. If I am fishing wet fly I use it ungreased and grease it when changing to a floating fly.

As I have tried to demonstrate in the sketch of a typical pool, dry fly fishing can be done either upstream or downstream, or if you like, round the clock.

The thing that really determines which way to fish, and from which bank if you have the choice, is the direction of the wind. Only a fool fishes downstream into the teeth of an upstream wind given any choice in the matter. When dry fly fishing, the choice is easy. If the wind is upstream—fish upstream, if it's downstream—fish downstream. Wet fly fishing by its very nature is easier fished across and downstream so there is only the choice of banks to be considered on a windy day.

Whichever style of fishing you propose using study the wind and use it to the best advantage. If you are right handed and the wind is downstream fishing from the right bank will keep your cast down wind of you. If the wind is upstream, casting from the left bank will keep the cast clear of you. Vice versa applies to the left hander.

If you are on a controlled beat, and you have to fish each pool working the beat downstream, and there is an upstream wind, start from the tail. If you cannot do that then start from the head and bring the back cast over the down wind shoulder, to prevent the fly coming round one side of your head, and the weight of the line round the other and dragging the hook into your face or eye; and always wear glasses. If your sight is perfect, use plain industrial glasses. Salmon fishing in a wind is a very dangerous game no matter what style of fishing you are doing. The winds in the Highlands of Scotland are notorious, for changing direction at the critical moment.

The beauty of Yellow Dolly fishing, is that you can fish in any direction and on any type of water.

Having read La Branche's book on his experiences fishing a dry fly, I've been intrigued by the direct conflict in our respective ways of fishing the greased fly. He is most emphatic that there should be no drag on the fly, and he went to great lengths to achieve this. He also developed a style of casting to put a right or left hand bend in his leader to allow the fly to float briefly with the current, without drag, when fishing fast water.

I am fairly confident that the idea that drag on a fly is off-putting to a salmon developed from La Branche's strong feelings on the subject fuelled no doubt by his trout fishing experiences.

A dry fly tied with a palmer hackle floats when dry and sinks like a wet fly when drowned. Therefore dry fly fishermen go to great lengths to keep their fly dry. An upstream presentation is the easiest way to keep the fly floating, it is only one step on to abhor drag which would drown the fly. Salmon were taken on a free floating fly and because the fly was fished without drag the myth was established that drag on the fly must be avoided.

I fish by putting movement on the fly, very seldom letting the fly float with the current other than the first few feet after the cast. I do vary the pace of the fly and mend line in fast water to stop the fly being dragged under. My idea is to make the fly have a movement independent of the flow and I am certain that this contrary movement is what induces the fish to take.

La Branche used large flies without drag and I use small flies with drag. Whether a large fly floating on the tackle tips appears smaller to the fish and a small fly moving on the surface appears larger so that they have a similar impact on the fish to induce a take is the only theory I can offer that accommodates the difference in size.

La Branche did his fishing on rivers with a very short season that were, from his own description, packed with fish, so that he was fishing over a greater number of fresh fish, and fresh fish, particularly grilse, I have found will take a free floating fly; but for everyone that will, many more will take a moving fly.

The Yellow Dolly is a very small fly. The larger $\frac{5}{8}''$ fly moves fish earlier in the season. By the end of May, it catches fish, but as the season goes on, the smaller fly, $\frac{1}{2}''$ or $\frac{3}{8}''$, catches more. It is always best to start fishing with a slightly larger than the norm for the day, then there's a chance of moving a fish, where as if the fly is too small for the day the fish will not move to the fly and a potential taking fish is passed over. Therefore, it is better to fish with the bigger fly that will make the fish show, and then concentrate on trying to catch it. If you fail, at least you know where he is, and can try later with a different approach. Should it move to the fly fished downstream and a change of fly does not catch it then try later fishing upstream.

Stealth and concealment will undoubtedly put more fish into the bag.

The fisherman that studies the pool and works out his approach, allowing for the very acute vision of the salmon, will have more success than the man who just follows the path to the river, wades in, and starts to fish. All my observations of salmon lead me to the believe that their eyesight is as sharp as any Heron or cock pheasant. Any approach, particularly in low water conditions that does not allow for this is doomed to failure.

Dry fly fishing for salmon requires the same skills as deer stalking. Consider the wind, study the ground, make full allowance for the senses of the quarry, and above all, have patience. When stalking, if you put it together correctly, and reach a comfortable place to take the shot from, then you've only to hold the rifle steady, and take the shot, and the beast is on its way to the larder.

With salmon fishing, having put it all together correctly and reached the right spot unseen, and moved the fish with the fly, I can equate the position with stalker who has got into position for the shot, but can only see the horns of the stag.

You both have to exercise patience until you can put the final touch to the hunt.

That is what the sport is; hunting and the purpose is to outwit the quarry in its territory, and put it into the larder.

Salmon can't be finished with a bullet when fly fishing, and there is no way of making it open its mouth, unless the salmon wants to.

It's at this point that the real fascination of Yellow Dolly fishing grips you. The fish is there. It's moved to the fly. How do you induce it to open its mouth? How do you transform interest into aggression that ultimately makes the fish seize the fly?

This is what I want the fisherman to experience. To see a salmon's head come out of the water behind his fly. To see its neb showing behind the fly as he follows it. To see him send up a bow wave as he moves to the fly, and the flash and swirl as he turns short. To see it put its chin on top of the fly and drown it. To see him hurl himself out of the water and crash down on top of the fly, and the most spectacular of all, to see a fish come with a bow wave from yards away, and in the last yard come right on to the top of the water, with jaws wide open, and charge the fly. When you have seen this, you'll believe that it's aggression that makes a salmon take a fly.

Reading this, you may think it's April 1st, but it is not. Believe me, these are the many ways you will see salmon behave when confronted by this little impudent fly intruding into his territory.

During all these and many other manoeuvres, keep your eyes glued on the fly and the leader. When the fly disappears, he might have taken it. If the leader or line moves, he has taken it. Lift the rod and tighten the line, this will set the hook. He doesn't need any striking, the weight of the fish will do it all. You will click a few fish and feel the weight of others. These have just been caught by a hook point in the skin of the mouth. Once you feel the weight and have still got him on after the first rush, you have every chance of landing him, unless you are too hard in the way you play him.

If you have not had much experience in playing salmon, and wonder how much weight you can put on a fish, get a friend to hold the leader and run away from you, and then run towards you, and make a few jerky tugs to give you the feel of a salmon shaking its head. A rod held at right angles to the pull of a fish only puts a pressure of 2 to 3 lbs. on the fish and that's ample to tire him out.

Your friend will not be able to simulate a fish jumping out of the water for you to practise dropping the rod at the jump of the fish, but his antics will help when you do have a fish on the end of the line.

There's only one other point to make. When a fish has moved at your fly, and you have gone through your armoury of tricks to induce the fish to take, and the fish is not showing any further interest, you will suddenly get the feeling that he's not going to take. Leave him. There is nothing to be gained by pestering him. Go away and come back to him later with a different approach. It is possible that you frightened him with line flash, or line splash, or you were seen.

PLATE 7

Duncan Leslie casting from a sitting position, well concealed

Rob Wilson achieves concealment by standing well back

PLATE 8

Susan Rattray fishing the head of the 'Pulpit Pool'

Tailing a fish
correctly

Grip the fish with finger and thumb avoid collapsing the tail with
the other fingers

5

Fishing a Sub-surface Fly

I have dealt with dry fly fishing for salmon in the previous chapter in a way that explains my method to all fishermen. However, I do feel that those who have not fished all that much for salmon require a little more help to catch a summer fish before attempting the dry fly. I know that given certain conditions, salmon can be caught in low water when greased line sub-surface flies get no response from the salmon. The angler on holiday most probably has not had the opportunities to acquire such experience, and make the best of his opportunities. Therefore, with those less practised in mind, I shall explain in a simple way greased line fishing for summer salmon with a sub-surface fly.

To be successful in any field sport, it is essential to know as much as possible about the habits and actions of the quarry. The more experiences we have, the easier it is to anticipate the behaviour of the animal we are pursuing in this instance, the salmon.

Most fishermen know that a salmon returns to the river of its birth to spawn and not to feed. This immediately makes its behaviour different from the brown trout, therefore the fisherman should not view a salmon from a trout fishing angle. Trout lie in all kinds of places throughout the length of the river, in a constant search for food, and always ready to dart for cover if danger threatens.

A salmon enters the river of its birth not to feed, but to spawn. The early salmon can spend nearly 12 months in the river without feeding, patiently waiting for November and spawning time. By June, the early fish will have moved well up river and with the

higher water temperatures surmounted all the temperature bar-
riers. The grilse and summer salmon entering the river from June
onwards will swim non stop up river to the middle and upper
beats so quickly, that they will still have sea-lice on them. The
greatest number of salmon will be found in these middle and
upper beats. The main beats which held the spring fish will not
fish so well in summer, therefore, the fisherman is well advised
to seek the middle and upper beats. These beats will be on the
upper reaches and tributories of the main river, and carry less
water. They are best recognised as spate rivers, quickly affected
by dry and wet spells.

The salmon move up these smaller rivers on every rise of water,
and as they do so, are described as running fish. It is these running
fish that I shall start with.

A salmon moving upstream can travel many miles in one day,
or just move from one pool to the next. Salmon are very seldom
caught while they are actually moving upstream. It is when they
stop to rest that they are very susceptible to a fly.

During the running period at the height of a spate, and as the
river starts to fall the better taking lies are in the tail of the pool,
and the fisherman should concentrate more on the tail in the
smooth draw of water immediately above the rough water. As
the spate runs off and the water level drops, the fish cease to
run and settle into the pools, then they will be found in the lies
at the head of the pool, and in the slow deep flow in the middle.
If the pool is deep and canal like, fish will lie close to the bank
on the side brushed by the main current.

Most rivers have named pools, and it is fairly certain that these
pools were named because they hold fish. They should be studied
carefully for boils on the surface indicating a stone or boulder
large enough to offer comfortable lodgings for a salmon. All these
obstructions in the tail, middle or head of a pool are possible lies
where the salmon might be found.

Fishermen are confused by the surface of the river reflecting light. This shining sheen conceals the contours of the river bed, and encourages fishermen to imagine fish in all manner of places. I have seen nice streamy water all of six inches deep being fished because it looked attractive, with its nice rippling silvery surface; but salmon do not frequent such shallow places. They require a depth of water for security, and deeper water close by to flee to. They require a flow of water to face into and breathe, and shelter from the main force of the current. The higher the temperature of the water, the higher up the current in the neck of the pool the fish will lie.

Streamy runs two or three feet deep will hold salmon, but they are best avoided by the holiday angler unless he receives expert guidance as to whether they hold fish or not. So much time can be wasted fishing water that doesn't hold fish. Those unfamiliar to the water are well advised to concentrate on the named pools. Even if they cannot recognize any of the lies, they will cover a fish just by fishing the water.

So to greased line fishing.

The rod, reel and line described previously for fishing a Yellow Dolly are ideal for the greased line fishing of sub-surface low water flies. The term 'greased line' goes back to the time of Arthur Wood when he fished with a silk line that required greasing to make the line float. A more apt description is 'floating line'. The modern synthetic fly lines do away with the drudgery of line drying and re-greasing every morning before fishing. Now you can come home, put the rod in the rack, and it is ready for the next day. The only difference between the equipment for sub-surface flies and floating flies is the leader, which, for sub-surface flies, is not greased.

I go fishing for summer salmon with exactly the same tackle as I use for fishing a Yellow Dolly. A nine foot rod, a floating line, 6 or 8 lb. nylon for leaders, and summer flies. With the use of Mucilin and Yellow Dollies, I can change quickly to a floating fly when the opportunity presents itself.

From June to September, the temperature of the water is from 50° to the middle 60's°, and salmon will rise up to a fly fished just under the surface. It is the time when a fly rod comes into its own. To cast a floating line is a pleasure. The line can be lifted easily off the water and cast with the minimum of effort. A great contrast to the hauling out of a sinking line and its huge lure which spring fishing demands.

If the river to be fished is fairly wide, then thigh waders may be required to get within casting distance of the lies. I personally avoid waders if I can, preferring to walk in comfort, and I make quite an effort at times to reach a lie, even going to the extreme of taking off my boots and stockings to wade. I like walking in dry boots.

The one question I am asked more than any other is 'What fly should I put on?' A very important question indeed. The fly is the thing that must attract the salmon and make him want to take it in his mouth. If the fly does not do that, then how on earth can we catch a fish? We cannot. The object of all fishing is to make the fish open its mouth and take the hook, whether we use bait, lure or a natural fly. So what fly? I could ramble on for page upon page with ifs and buts, whys and wherefores, and the angler would be no wiser, and most probably totally confused. Therefore, I shall treat it in the most simple and straight forward way that works in practice.

Take the temperature of the water when you arrive at the water's edge. Then sit down and look at the river. Is it clear or dirty? Is it high or low? After a few moments you decide it is clear and of normal height, with a water temperature of 52°. The choice is simple, be we in Scotland, Ireland, England or Wales, a $\frac{3}{4}''$ long aluminium tube dressed with hair and a size 10 treble hook is the right size of fly. If you use low water doubles, then a size 4 will be perfect.

I prefer flies lightly dressed so that the body shows through the dressing, and the hair extends just beyond the hook. The pattern of fly is the angler's choice.

Most fishermen have a favourite pattern, the colour appeals and they have caught fish on it. Or the gillie recommends the local fancy, or the chap in the pub caught a fish last week on a 'deadly demon'.

If you are new to salmon fishing, and have no ideas about patterns and no friendly fishermen to advise you, then go to the local fishing tackle shop and buy three 'Blue Charms' or 'Hairy Marys' tied on low water double hooks in sizes 4, 6, 8, 10 and 12. Fifteen flies in all and you have all that is required to catch salmon from June to September. The reason for three flies of each size is to allow for the losses in trees, grass, bracken, heather, and for hook points broken on boulders. So watch your back cast.

One of the great pleasures of salmon fishing is sitting or lolling watching the pool and all the life that goes on in and out of the water. The light reflecting off the water shows the currents, the swirls and boils, the back eddies and the smooth glides that make this pool slightly different to all the other pools. Reflected light is the biggest single problem for all fishermen. It disguises the river bed, it conceals the depth of water, it hides the fish and leaves the fisherman groping in the dark.

Without reflected light, all would be revealed, every boulder, every fish, and the anticipation and charm of fishing would be lost.

It is so pleasant sitting watching the flies hovering and darting over the water, trout rising, the dipper bobbing on his favourite stone, the sheer comfort and joy of a summer's day by the river. But I must make an effort and suggest how to fish the pool with a floating line.

The concealment aspect of fishing is ignored by a lot of

fishermen, and they do catch fish. They would catch more if they took more care. However, I am not going to start you fishing by having you crawl and then cast from a sitting position. We are going to conceal ourselves by going some ten yards upstream of the head of the pool. The broken water in the head of the pool will hide us from the fish. Greased line fishing for salmon is exactly the same as wet fly fishing for trout. The cast is made across and downstream. When trout fishing, I would use a floating line and a ten foot ungreased leader with three flies. Salmon fishing, I use a ten or eleven foot ungreased leader with one fly. The breaking strain of the leader is slightly stronger for salmon, and for a novice I think 10 or 12 lbs. would be ideal. We wade into the water if it is necessary to cover the holding stream in the head of the pool. The easy way if fishing with a floating line, is to fish the water and not worry about the lies.

If salmon are in the river and the water is near normal, then the salmon will have stopped running and the majority will be in the holding pools, which on most rivers, are named pools. Even on tiny spate rivers, pools that hold salmon are named. This tendency of salmon to settle into pools simplifies the selection of suitable fishing areas. Our pool has salmon in, I saw one bulge the surface. Start fishing by drawing line off the reel and cast a short line to drop the fly just above the rough water and let the current carry it round. Continue to fish by lengthening the line three feet at every cast, and fish in the same way as I described, fishing down stream with a dry fly, lengthening line at every cast. You will cover the water with the fly in arcs, each one three feet greater in radius than the last.

By doing this, the first view the salmon has of you will be your fly, and you will automatically cover every fish. Fishing with an ever lengthening line suddenly brings the moment when you feel that you cannot comfortably cast any further without making a mess of your casting. Do not try, shorten the line by a yard or so, and move a yard downstream, between each cast. Whether wading or bank fishing, keep clear of any stream that could hold fish, you do not want to frighten them, they could disturb other fish. Fishermen have an irresistible urge to fish the opposite bank's water. For some peculiar reason they always assume the fish to be lying at the other side of the river. If you took a mile of river and drew a line down the centre of it, 50% of the fish would be on one side of it, and 50% on the other. So why frighten 50 fish to cover 50 fish?

Casting for distance is another urge for most fishermen. Forget it. Cast a comfortable length of line and you will cover just as many fish in the day with more chance of catching them. What is a good casting distance? I read a lot of fishing magazines which are full of fishing stories describing 25 and 30 yard casts and aerialising the whole of the fly line etc. I do not doubt the writers ability to cast such distances, but I question the necessity for it. With a ten foot rod rated AFTM 7–8 and Weight Forward No. 7 line, I can cast 24 yards of fly line without false casting. People who use the double haul method of casting can cast further, and on average take four false casts before every true cast. So take heart, distance is not a necessity, my casts at known lies are no more than 15 yards of fly line, plus the length of the leader. Generally speaking, I fish with about 12 yards of fly line when fishing in normal summer conditions. The majority of fish are lying in the streamy runs at the head of the pool during the warm days of summer, and they are the ones for the newcomer to salmon fishing to concentrate upon.

Fishing down the pool with a nice length of line, the fly swimming just under the surface, the current is doing all the work and the only help you may need to give is a slight mend of line into the current to remove the downstream curve of line which makes the fly race across the current. Mending a line, is the simple flick of the rod tip which lifts the line lying on the water nearest the rod away from him, and by so doing, removes the curve in the line. It is a lot easier to control 10 yards of line and make the fly swim in a manner attractive to fish, than it is with 20 yards of line between you and the fly. When the fly has swum across the current and comes into the slacker water, bring the fly up the edge of the current for a few yards by stripping line through the index finger of the rod hand, and then lift into the next cast and shoot the slack line. By moving a yard between casts the run is soon fished down. Carry on as far as the current continues to fish the fly properly. If you have been careful, and not waded more than knee deep, and kept well clear of the edge of the current, then you can give it a rest for ten minutes, then fish it down once more.

If nothing has moved at the fly after the second run down, move on to the next pool and go through the same procedure in the next pool. One thing I must stress, the further away you are from the streams that hold fish the greater your chance of an offer.

A very important point generally raises its head at this stage. Should I change my fly? The answer is a definite NO. You have on the right size of fly for the prevailing conditions. If the salmon is in any mood to take the fly, the one you have on is the one that will move him. The time to consider a change of fly is when a fish comes to the fly and doesn't take it. Then change the fly to the next size down. In your case, change the size 4 for a size 6 low water double. When a fish moves at the fly and does not take, pause for a minute, and cast at him again. If he does not rise to this cast, do not cast at him again. Either slowly retreat to the bank, or stay perfectly still and change the fly without winding any line on the the reel. This ensures the right length for the next cast with the new fly. If you opt to stay still, take your time changing the fly, there is no urgency, a settled fish does not change his lodgings.

To cast the new fly, trail the line on the edge of the current to draw out line so that the very first cast is made to the exact spot of the previous cast that moved the fish. I would recommend the less experienced fisherman to move quietly out of the river or retire from the bank, and return to where he was sitting before starting to fish. There he can change his flies in comfort without fear of disturbing the fish. Start again at the top of the run and fish all the way down with the smaller fly. You have every chance of hooking him.

That then is the essence of greased line fishing, and it will catch summer salmon. There are many little nuances one can add to the style and presentation, and little tricks one acquires as the years go by. It's fun finding out these by oneself instead of having every little thing explained in detail.

I run a 'Sporting Week' once a year for a few people to catch a salmon and stalk a stag. One year I had two Australian lady schoolteachers, who had a desire to catch a salmon, and had travelled all the way from Australia to the north of Scotland to participate in my sporting week. One was 50 and the other 55 years of age, and neither had even held a fishing rod, let alone fished. On the Monday, they were taught to cast, the next day they were shown how to fish four pools, and on the Wednesday they were left to fish the four pools on their own, with the parting advice to keep back from the edge of the bank. The youngest caught her first salmon that afternoon, and the other caught hers the next day.

To end the story, the weather turned cold on the Thursday afternoon, and the stags came down from the hills during the evening to feed in the Strath. The rut had just started and the bigger stags had gone to the hinds. A bunch of about 200 stags were very close to the lodge, so I took the Australian ladies to see them, and they took dozens of photographs, during the course of which they changed their minds about wanting to shoot a stag.

They still wanted to go stalking, but only to take photographs. A certain number of stags must be shot in the limited time available before winter, so it was decided that they would go with the second stalker, who would take the rifle and the whole proceedings would be carried out in earnest.

That evening, two tired and bedraggled school ma'ams returned deliriously happy with excitement. 'They' had shot the heaviest stag on the Forest. 'They' had lain for an hour in a bog with water running in at their necks and out of their trousers. 'They' had crawled for miles pushing deer dung with their noses, and finally, 'they' had laid unseen amongst all the deer until the stag got up and instantly dropped dead. 'They' had such a struggle to load it and bring it home. What a week!

The point of this little story, is listen to the advice of the professional—ghillie or stalker, he knows his river or hills like the back of his hand. If salmon are in the pools and the right size of fly is being used and the ghillie's advice is followed then even the novice will be nearly as successful as the expert. The expert has the advantage, because he spends less time fishing unproductive water. The salmon, however, is only attracted by the fly, and not by who maybe on the other end.

I can just imagine the salmon saying 'I'm having this one, she's blonde'.

Which reminds me of the dear old lady who came to fish. She used a 7'6" cane dry fly rod, a mere wand of a rod. She was found late one afternoon sitting by the pool, very near to tears. She had hooked a salmon in the middle of the pool, and the first hour it had swum majestically up and down the pool, resting for a while, and then touring the pool again. This had completely tired her out, and she sat down and waited for someone to come along. She was not going to leave her fish. She and the fish had declared a truce, he returning to his lie, and her sitting down, and they had been like this for half an hour. Help arrived in the form of another lady with a more determined character. She promptly stirred the majestic monster out of its bed, and after a few quicker tours of the pool, popped the net in front of him, and he weighed $12\frac{1}{2}$ lbs. The dear old lady was so proud that her little rod had caught such a monster.

To return to greased line fishing and flies.

Having said that one pattern in five sizes will serve from June to September, it only remains for me to give some guide as to when to use each size of fly.

WATER TEMPERATURE AND SUB-SURFACE FLY SIZES

Water Temp.	Low Water Double	Alum. Tube
52°	4	$\frac{3}{4}''$
54°	6	
56°	8	$\frac{1}{2}''$
58°	8	
60°	10	
64°	12	

If the river is above normal height, clear, and fish are running, and the correct temperature size of fly has brought no response, put on a size larger. Equally, in the other direction if the river is in a low water state, try the next size down. This simple approach of only two fly sizes in one pattern, allows the fisherman to concentrate on the pools without the nagging doubt that his fly is the wrong one.

Salmon are creatures of moods sometimes (most times), lying immovable and impervious to all our attempts to get their attention. Other times their response can be electrifying. One thing, they are never asleep. The fish will see your fly no matter how tiny it is, or how rough the water, and when he wants it, he will take it with absolute precision. A salmon never misses the fly when he wants it.

When he comes up and does not take, he's interested, but not in an aggressive enough mood to take a fly that is perhaps a shade too big.

If the temperature is above 54° and a smaller size does not make him take, then the ideal moment to try a Yellow Dolly is with you. Grease the leader and the Yellow Dolly, and fish it in the same way as your sub-surface fly, only this time keep it right on top of the water. I am fairly certain you will get a response to the Yellow Dolly, and whether you catch him or not, you will be caught by the Yellow Dolly.

6

Temperature and Conditions

Understanding water temperature is the secret to successful salmon Fishing, and is a very neglected subject. Most authorities on salmon fishing mention temperature as the change from sinking lines and big flies to floating lines and small flies. A temperature of 48° is quoted as change over time, and that's the subject of temperature dealt with.

John Ashley-Cooper, in his book *A Line on Salmon*, devotes a chapter to temperature and breaks it down into sections. Reg Ryghyni in his book *Advanced Salmon Fishing* also lays stress on temperature and relates size to temperature. Both contain the basic information on which to build to be a successful salmon fisherman.

My experience of temperature, is that actual water temperature at the time of fishing, dictates tactics.

If I start with spring fishing, when the water temperature can be 34° for weeks on end in February and March, with the line freezing in the rings, and definitely not Yellow Dolly time. However, let the clouds break and the sun come through, and the water temperature will creep up to 36°, and this 2° rise will affect the fish and readily explain why midday suddenly produces a fish.

Towards the end of March, sunshine has more effect on the water, and the water temperature can move through 3 degrees from say 36° to 39°, and the 4″ fly goes down to a 3″.

During April, the water slowly increases its basic temperature day by day, and each day is generally at its lowest temperature around sunrise. The increase throughout the day is dependent on the amount of sunshine, and/or the thickness of cloud cover.

At the beginning of May the morning temperatures can be 46°, and a sunk fly is used. After lunch, the temperature can be 52°, and a floating line with a $\frac{3}{4}''$ tube fly will catch fish.

A water temperature of 52° has a great deal of significance for me, it is the start of summer fishing.

My river in Sutherland, does not get a Spring run of salmon because of two falls which form a very effective temperature barrier. The first fall is a lift of about 12 ft. split into two 6 ft. falls just a few yards apart. Salmon will negotiate these when the water temperature reaches 48° and if there is fresh water they will run to the foot of the second fall. This fall is a formidable barrier, with a lift of 14 ft. Many years ago it was a proper waterfall which blocked the passage of fish until part of the lip was hewn away. Now it is a raging torrent let into the side of the fall which the salmon will not attempt to go over until the water temperature is higher than 52°.

One year, I spent three consecutive days watching this fall when the water was right for the fish to run. At 4.00 pm on the third day the sun, which had shone from lunchtime, lifted the water temperature from 46° to just over 52°, and at 4.30 pm the fish which had been milling round the pool for three days started to run the fall. The following year the fish arrived at the foot of the main fall when the temperature reached 48° but the weather was not kind. For over a week it was cold and overcast and the water temperature varied only between 46° and 50° and the salmon waited below the falls. The water was perfect for the fish to run with frequent little freshets but the sun remained hidden. It was ten days before the sun broke through, the temperature rose and the fish went over the falls.

Temperature has a very meaningful effect on salmon. I relate it to the Bumble Bee that cannot fly until its flying muscles are warmed sufficiently by the sun so that it can beat its wings fast enough to develop the power to fly. Likewise with the salmon, which takes its body temperature from the water, until its muscles reach 52° it cannot develop enough sustained power and speed to attempt the second fall. It also explains to me why spring salmon hardly show, and summer salmon with more energetic bursts throw themselves out of the water.

On my river, the main source of water is from two connected lochs nearly five miles in total length. The many burns gather the water from the water shed, and these pour into the loch, the outfall of which is the head of the river. During a period of heavy rain, the lochs act as a reservoir, and as the level rises, impound a considerable amount of water. The rise and fall at the head of the river is therefore very much slowed down, and the water is always clean. Also the temperature is relatively low and is slow to rise through the day.

As the water goes downstream, numerous burns enter the river, and these rise and fall very rapidly during and after a spate. They also bring in a lot of debris, and at the height of a spate, discolour the river water. During the spate, and for a short while afterwards, the temperature is at its lowest and the water discoloured by the peat. This warrants the use of 2″ flies, with a water temperature around 46–48°.

However, within 24 hours the burns fine down and the water gradually clears, the temperature rises to 50–52°, and 1″ brass tubes are effective for a while. Some two or three miles further downstream, $\frac{3}{4}$″ and $\frac{1}{2}$″ tubes are more effective, when the sun breaks through lifting the temperature.

It is very interesting the way the water temperature at midday increases the further down river I go, along its six mile length. For example, one year, on the 27th of May, I recorded a temperature of 48° at the head of the river, 50° two miles downstream, and 53° six miles downstream. At sunrise, this variation is only

a matter of 2° over the six miles. With the advance of the day
the burns and the river warm a lot quicker than the loch, due
to the sun shining on the water as it flows over the shallow gravel
runs between the pools. By end of June, there can be a 6° variation
along the length of the river, coupled with an 8° rise through
the day, giving a 14° variation over the day. This is considerable,
and has a marked influence on the size of flies used throughout
the day. Indeed I have recorded an increase during the day of
18° from 58° to 76°.

Without a thermometer, I changed flies going smaller through
the day. Now after much recording I realise the extent of the
change and am a lot more extreme in my fly changes, even though
the river level does not fall much during the day. I can start fishing
in the morning with a 1″ brass tube and finish the day with a
size 12 double—which I actually did one day, and caught ten
fish. The ninth I took on a Yellow Dolly after he had moved to
a $\frac{1}{2}$″ Badger. The tenth also refused the Badger. As I was tying
on the Yellow Dolly I remembered the size 12 double I had tied
to represent a smaller version of my $\frac{1}{2}$″ Badger, I put it on instead
of the Yellow Dolly and the salmon took it. I had nine fish on
Badgers of varying sizes, and one on a Yellow Dolly.

You are now going to ask 'Why only one on a Yellow Dolly?',
and the answer is I fish with ordinary flies to avoid any self decep-
tion about the Yellow Dolly. When I find a taking fish that I cannot catch with ordinary flies, I can try and winkle it out with
a Yellow Dolly. Nine times out of ten it works.

I am firmly convinced that size and temperature are related.
Why a salmon should take a 4″ lure when the water temperature
is 33° and a $\frac{1}{2}$″ lure at 60°, I cannot explain, but as the water
temperature goes up the size of the lure comes down. Whether
it is that the salmon, who becomes more active as the temperature
goes up also becomes more perceptive and aware of his surroundings, so that the lure size related to temperature creates the same

PLATE 9

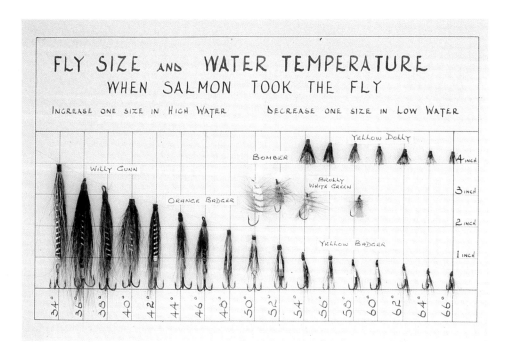

This chart will help the angler to catch salmon and remove some of the mystique from fly selection. One can switch from sinking to floating line somewhere between 40° and 48°

The loch at the head of the river influences temperature and moderates the spates

PLATE 10

One of the two lower falls which salmon will run at 48°

General view of the main fall

View of the cleft hewn into the main fall which salmon will negotiate when the temperature exceeds 52°

degree of aggressive feeling, I do not know. I do know the way he responds indicated that it does, and I fish accordingly. All creatures are individuals, and yet have similar responses within the breed. Walk along a road, and when someone is walking towards you and is aware of you, look up, and he will look up in response to your action. Salmon respond to the right size of lure. Forget about all the odd exceptions that are trotted out, such as 3″ lures in low water. Experiments can wait.

My list of temperatures and fly sizes is set out in the form of a chart and it is based on salmon that I have caught, and salmon that I have seen respond to the fly. To make it interesting I have taken a photograph showing the actual flies used and the temperature when the fish took the fly. They plot a very even line on the chart and show a clear relationship between size and temperatures. When I was plotting the chart I endeavoured to plot a reducing curve but I found that three straight lines of different angles plotted much better than a curve. The interesting thing was the temperature at the change of angle, 38° and 54° both of which are significant to me. In spring when fishing very cold water fish will not move for a fly and it must be right on his nose for him to take. When the water temperature increases to 38° then fish will begin to move to the fly.

A temperature of 54° signals the moment when the fish will come up for a surface fly. This confirmation was really very pleasing and I've incorporated the lines in the photograph on plate 9.

To fish a Yellow Dolly successfully, requires a temperature of 54°, and to fish a sub surface fly on a greased line requires a temperature of 50°. In both cases, a fish could be caught at lower temperatures.

I personally would not bother trying. My experience is that in the case of the Yellow Dolly, I would do better with a ½″ tube fly, and at 48° the sunk fly would do better than a sub-surface fly. Whenever the water temperature goes over 50°, floating line tactics have a better chance of success. When I am salmon fishing a temperature of 52° means a $\frac{3}{4}''$ Aluminium Tube, 56° a $\frac{1}{2}''$ Aluminium Tube or a Yellow Dolly. 60° a size 12 double or a small Yellow Dolly.

Height of water doesn't matter—temperature does. That last sentence explains salmon fishing, and sea trout fishing for that matter.

Think of low water in high summer, when the advice is—get up early because the first 2 hours after sunrise offers the best chance of a fish. Why? Because the water temperatures can drop 10° overnight, and be between 56° or 60° at sunrise, ideal for a small fly. 70° at midday and a bright sun tests a small Yellow Dolly, and a size 12 double hasn't a hope.

Buy and use a thermometer, and become an advanced salmon fisher.

One thing I have learned about salmon fishing. There is always the exception, but the degree of variation to the norm is never great.

There are two other influences which I think work on the salmon, and I am a great believer in them.

The first is a rising glass. A falling glass to me means unresponsive fish, particularly in low water.

After a spate, the glass generally rises for a few days, and the fishing is good. After a few more days as the river falls, barometrical pressure takes over and affects the fishing.

The second and major influence is wind.

I love a windy day that puts a cockle on the pools. I positively delight in an upstream gale that puts a wave on the flat pools and batters wave upon wave at the rough water. In such conditions, with a rising glass, salmon can be caught in the very driest of summers, providing they are in the pools.

Wind cockling the water helps to conceal the angler in low water conditions, and by using a stalkers approach, enables the fly to be presented to the fish without the fish being aware of the angler. Oxygen content may have an influence on fish, but it is too complicated for me. I can explain and anticipate the salmon's desire to attack my flies by observing temperature, atmospheric pressure and wind.

I think that clarity of water has more influence on the size of fly than the height of the water. Having said all this about temperature, pressure, wind and clarity, there are the odd occasions when they all work against the fisherman, and then nothing will induce a fish to open its mouth, and this state can go on for a few days.

It sometimes happens when the river appears to be in very good order, and by the appearance of the river fish should be caught; but they will not take, and the only reaction the fish makes is to leave its lie when it becomes frightened. A tap on the glass that night usually shows a fall in atmospheric pressure. Then I leave the river alone and do something else, or go fishing for brownies in the loch.

I have been experimenting for the last few years fishing with tube flies and low water flies as the river falls, and going onto a Yellow Dolly when either a fish moved to a sub-surface fly and couldn't be caught with normal tactics; or there was no offer from a fish, when I was certain there was a fish in the lie.

When the river turns over and starts to fall, it can be dirty with weeds and debris for the first 24 hours which make salmon unresponsive. The second and third days after the spate offer very good fishing and ordinary flies catch better than Yellow Dollies. From the fourth day on as the river fines down the Yellow Dolly comes into its own, and will move fish when ordinary flies will not.

When to fish the Yellow Dolly? When the water temperature is 54° or more. When the fish became difficult in low water and you have a fish that you cannot catch. When you are proficient enough to practice the supreme way of catching a salmon.

Many people I know have caught salmon with a Yellow Dolly, others just cannot grasp the technique of fishing a floating fly. They have a mental block that prevents them changing from the conventional way of salmon fishing.

They represent my mental picture of a typical salmon fisherman fishing low water in the middle of summer. Standing there like an advert for salmon fishing in eighteen inches of water wearing chest waders, sixteen feet of rod held low over the water, loop of line hanging from their rod hand, other arm on hip and yards of line dangling across the river. They really do enjoy themselves and that is what fishing is about enjoying oneself. After the initial attempt to teach them I leave them to do their own thing. When fishing in low water the most important thing of all, and I cannot stress it enough is to remain out of the sight of the fish.

When the river is low or very low during periods of drought the fish are settled in the pools. In this settled state they are aware of every aspect of their surroundings. The slightest change in their scene will alert them and send them darting downstream to fling themselves out of the water 30 yards away from their lie.

Some fishermen when they see a fish show like that promptly go and cast at the spot not realising that their presence has frightened the fish out of its lie and whilst they are busy thrashing at the spot the fish has returned quietly to its lie in the current.

When this happens frequently on a pool the fish become as scary as seatrout and are impossible to catch.

The merest flash of a fly line will send them down the pool before the first cast touches the water.

Some pools are so lacking in cover that when creeping into a place to cast from, fish can be frightened in very low water conditions when there is no wind to ruffle the water. The unfrightened fish if he only sees the fly and not the fisherman will respond by at least coming up to inspect it and this show of interest indicates a possible taking fish.

Some of the best fishing I have experienced has been during long periods of summer drought. A gale blowing on the flat pools stirs the fish out of their trance. It has a similar affect to a drop of fresh water and the fish become keen to chase a surface fly buzzing across the waves.

Even on a day with little wind if the glass is high or rising the fish will respond to a dry fly as long as the fisherman keeps out of sight.

The rough water at the head of a pool is my favourite spot, tucked in to the side of the bank concealed from the fish I can have an amusing time trying to tempt an interested fish to open his mouth for one of a variety of flies I show him.

There is no doubt about the best time to catch fish. It is when the spate starts to run off and the water clears; then fish can be caught by anyone that can put a fly over a fish. There is no great skill in it. It is more a case of being in the right place at the right time with the right size of fly. That's why anyone that's keen enough to try can catch a salmon—children, old ladies, experts they all have a similar chance. The first person to cover a taking fish will catch it. Fortunately for the salmon the river does not remain in such a good state for long or there would not be many salmon left in the river.

The response of a salmon to a dry fly is visual and so thrilling when a great silver fish suddenly appears that I have to make a conscious effort to fish with an ordinary fly. Nearly every time I go salmon fishing during the summer I start with a Yellow Badger and unless I'm on one of my experimental days I switch to a Yellow Dolly whenever I move fish.

I fish a floating fly for the thrill of seeing the fish take and the challenge of catching a fish when all other ways fail. I even look forward with pleasure to low water and hot summers providing I've got fish in the river. It is the cream of salmon fishing and good for the grouse prospects.

7

Experiences

Having gone through the history of salmon dry fly, the creation of the Yellow Dolly, and how to fish it, I can best give other illustrations by telling a few stories.

'That reminds me' is one of my most used phrases and whenever I start talking, it soon pops to the surface. No doubt a sign of old age stalking me.

After I'd written the letters to Hugh Falkus, he rang up to say that he would be in the north of Scotland for a couple of days and would like to visit, and see the Yellow Dolly that I'd described, in action. Unfortunately, the river was in flood, it was the last week in September, and the prospects for dry fly fishing were hopeless. However, because there wouldn't be another opportunity that year, and he wanted to take photographs of salmon lies and pools, he came to stay for the last few days of the season.

I have a pool that's long and flat, and even with a 2 foot spate in the river, it flows smoothly but swiftly. I said to him that we would go to this pool and I would show him how I would have fished a Yellow Dolly upstream in low water, if the river had been in good order and he'd arrived in summer.

We went to the pool and sat downstream of the first lie, and I described to him what I would do, then I cast and fished up

70

to the lie, covered it and nothing moved to the fly. I said the other lie was about 20 yds. further upstream, and in summer I could crawl from where we were sitting to the point from where I could fish. Hugh said 'Well let's do it as though it was summer.' On went the waterproof trousers, and we crawled. Hugh with his camera, his friend with his, and I with the rod. 'Now' I said, when we got there, 'I'll fish up to the lie which is under the far bank, and I'll lengthen at every cast until I cover it.' I started fishing and lengthening line at every cast. I was covering the lie, when much to my surprise, up came the fish as though it was the middle of summer, and took the fly like a big trout taking a Mayfly. I played the fish and finally tailed him.

Hugh then expressed a wish to go and see the Rock Pool where I once fished for a salmon for two hours, which moved at every change of fly, and yet I couldn't induce it to open its mouth and eventually, suffering from cramp, I gave him best and bid him good day.

When we arrived at the Rock Pool, I took one look and said there was no chance of using a dry fly. So Hugh asked if he could fish it down. 'Of course', said I. He put his rod up and put on a No. 2 lure of his own tying, and on the third cast, it was taken by a lively old cock fish.

Next morning, Hugh said he'd like a Yellow Dolly, and to go off on his own to fish it.

I showed him two pools on the Estate Map that might fish now the water had dropped a little over-night. He went to the first pool, did everything I had told him, and not a fish moved. The other pool was just a hundred yards downstream, and he went down to try it with no great feeling of anticipation. He cast his fly upon the water, and up came the fish and took it, and so he caught his first fish on a Yellow Dolly. I let him keep the fly as a pattern.

He wrote to me the following autumn, saying that he had tried a Yellow Dolly pattern with a spun deer hair head, and this had caught many fish. I also had a note from Stephen Riding, saying that he had seen the fly I had given Hugh, and he had tied some and caught two fish with them during his holidays in the north of Scotland. He was extremely pleased, as he caught the only fish taken on that particular river during his holidays.

I went to Connemara one July, to fish for salmon on the very good little river I mentioned earlier. It is famous for its sea trout, and holds quite a few salmon. Unfortunately, the river was very low, and no fish had been caught for over a fortnight. I arrived late on the Sunday, and was staying in a cottage by the river. On Monday morning, I was up bright and early and off for a quick stroll up the river before breakfast; with a rod, of course. The third pool on the beat has a brisk run of water into the pool, and the water is channelled on to one bank, and for about five yards the water hugs the bank before the flow disperses across the pool. With Yellow Dolly greased, I cast upstream, close under my bank. At about the third cast, up came a bonny fresh fish and took it first time. It did a sea trout performance round the pool, before I tailed him, knocked him on the head, and back for breakfast. Nothing else was caught that day.

That night at supper, my friend said that he had heard the suggestion that my fish might not have been caught in a fair manner; the tale emanating from a rather superior salmon fisherman, whose reputation was held in much awe by other lesser fishermen. 'Right', I said to my friend, 'let it be known that I shall have another fish before the week is out.' This was rather flying in the face of providence, but I knew there was another fish in the pool, and it ought to move into the lie, and providing it wasn't disturbed too much, I had a chance.

Next morning, again out before breakfast, and in an exact carbon copy, the same thing happened. I couldn't do it again during the remainder of the week, but I did have the only two fish caught that week. No doubt, the mighty fisherman is still saying that I snatched them, which rather appeals to my sense of humour. I like telling the truth in such a way that people think I am pulling their leg, but not in this book, it's all true.

The twelfth of August dawned one year, wet, windy and miserable. So much so that the start of the grouse shooting was cancelled. We do all our grouse shooting over pointers, and even though the dogs will work, that sort of day is not enjoyable, and we are not under any pressure to shoot, so the traditional supper would have to wait a day or so.

By lunchtime, there had been no improvement, so I suggested to my friend that we should go fishing, as the river was in good order for a salmon. We had a 4 mile walk across country to get to the lower pools, and by the time we arrived, it was threatening more and heavier rain, and the wind was a near howling gale. The pool we were going to fish was a deep pool very slow moving about a hundred yards long. The fish lie in the current along the far bank. There are no lies in the head of it, but a very good lie at the tail where a large boulder protrudes from the bank. My friend put on a Yellow Badger tied on a half inch aluminium tube with a dressing of a dozen long hairs and a yellow hackle.

I went half way up the pool to fish with a similar fly, casting across to the far bank. This requires a very long cast, shooting lots of line to drop the fly close in under the far bank.

The conventional way of fishing this pool is by backing up, which means casting across and downstream, and then taking two paces upstream to put movement on the fly as it swings slowly across the current. I find it just as effective to cast across and slightly upstream, and strip the line back, and then shoot the line again taking a pace upstream between casts.

After about half a dozen casts, a fish took the fly, and was on. I looked downstream to my friend, just in time to see him lift into a fish. After a spirited fight, I tailed a grilse and then went down to tail my friend's fish. After congratulating each other, I suggested he cast again at the rock, as it was a lie that quite often produced another fish. He did, and another fish moved at the fly, but didn't take him. After a few more casts he changed to a smaller fly, but the fish wouldn't come again. I asked if he would like to fish a Yellow Dolly. As he had never tried dry fly on salmon, and as the fish had not been frightened, it was an ideal opportunity for him to try it out. This he did, and the fish was most obliging. As soon as he pulled the fly over the lie, it came charging across the top of the water with its mouth open, but didn't take him. Another cast and it did the same thing. I told him to try once more and move the fly a little quicker, not hesitating waiting for the fish to take. He did, and the fish rose like a brownie and took the fly down. When it was safely on the bank, I asked him what he thought of Yellow Dolly fishing, and he shattered me by saying that he thought it was positively indecent making a salmon behave like a little trout.

The head stalker on the estate is a very strong wiry man, very determined, with piercing blue eyes which see things at a glance that I take ten minutes with a pair of 10x binoculars to find. He is a superb stalker and also a keen and capable fisherman; delights in trout fishing and pursues salmon with the same relentless zeal as foxes. He is the only person I've seen who because there was nothing better, fished with a 14 ft. glass fibre salmon rod one-handed all day in a boat, fishing for trout.

I had some fishing tenants one year who, because of the low water, were not catching any salmon. They asked the stalker's advice, and he told them to use small flies and stay well back from the bank. Each evening they came back empty handed and were told they were not taking enough care, and if they did, they would catch fish.

On the Friday, the tenants, who were reasonably competent fishermen, ganged up on the stalker, and bet him he couldn't catch a fish.

The next day, Saturday, was their last day. The stalker accepted the wager, and they all went down to the river. The pool he selected to fish was a long slow pool, which he knew held fish.

The main lies are tight under the far bank. It was a fine sunny morning, with odd patches of cloud and a wind blowing up the pool, creating a good ripple on the surface. He put up his 14 ft. rod with a floating line and tied on 18 ft. of 6 lb. nylon for a leader and a tiny tube. Leaving the fishermen well away from the pool, with strict instructions not to move, he went to the bottom end of the pool below the lowest lie. He stood some 8 yds. back from the bank and waited until a cloud obscured the sun. He cast across and downstream to get out line and when he had the right length of line, he cast the fly across and upstream to land it on the grass of the bank slightly upstream of the lie. Drawing line, the fly dropped into the water and he drew it over the lie and rose a fish, which didn't take him. The tenants said later, that he had only 18 casts in $1\frac{1}{2}$ hours, never casting unless the cloud obscured the sun. He had six rises from two fish and hooked and landed the second fish, and promptly went home. No doubt there was a twinkle in his blue eyes when he left them to put into practice what he'd been telling them all week. It nicely illustrates that fish can see, and in low water, fine and far, with concealment and awareness of the conditions is the only way to aproach salmon fishing.

Given cloud, wind and a rising glass, there is every chance of taking a fish, no matter how low the water, and how potted the fish.

1984 was a poor year for salmon fishing, no water and weeks of drought. Very good for the Mayfly fishing, the young grouse and the deer, but it caused a great upsurge in the Heather Beetle population which were rapidly eating their way through the low ground heather. A few salmon crept into the river in June and settled in the lower pools. Two fish were taken by the July tenants during the first week in July, and that was the total catch for the month. At the beginning of August, I had some friends staying, who reminded me that I had promised them salmon for supper. I noted this, said nothing, and watched the glass. Thursday dawned, cloudy, windy, and the glass was well up.'Come on', I said, 'We will go for a picnic.' They were non-fishing people, and a picnic down the river appealed to them. A little fire, barbequed sausages, tinker's tea etc.

I took a rod just in case!

I have a favourite pool in such low water conditions, with a coffin-like slab of stone in the current at the head of the pool; it is one of two lies that I know I can rely on to hold fish, and most probably, a taking fish. If there are only two fish in the entire river, one would be in each lie.

Having got the party merrily cooking sausages and enjoying themselves, I said that I would just pop off for a few minutes fishing. Two of them came with me to watch. The lie takes very little time to fish but the approach is rather difficult. The only way is to get into the middle of the river, and then go downstream, crouched as low as possible, very slowly to a rock, which is roughly 15 yds. directly upstream of the lie, and kneel in its shelter. To cover the lie, the fly must be cast into the slack water on the right-hand side of the current. The current picks up the line, and as the rod is held with the point on the left-hand side of the flow, a bag builds in the line, and in the final stage, drags the fly at right angles across the current, and over the lie. This I did, and up came an $8\frac{1}{2}$ lb. fish and took the fly. Supper was in the bag and I was credited with all the skills of a salmon charmer.

In fact, the major element was in knowing where the fish would be lying, and getting into position so that the only thing the fish saw was a little 'beasty' intruding into his territory. I believe that salmon lie downstream of rocks and obstructions, occasionally at the side, but very seldom in front. When they appear to be in front of a lie, if you look carefully, you will see another protrusion that he's in the lee of, or a depression in the gravel that gives shelter. When I seek shelter on the hill from the wind, I go into the lee of a rock, or into a depression. I never sit in front of a rock. Trout will lie in front of rock in mid-current on the fin watching for food, not resting. Some people may not agree, but my observations are that the majority of salmon lie behind obstructions. These may not be apparent to the fisherman. The contours of the river bottom are difficult to perceive from our distorted viewpoint, but the salmon can certainly find the sheltered lies. As I have said before there are always exceptions to any general statement about salmon. I have one lie in the river where a salmon does lie in front of a rock. It is a large cone shaped rock and when it is covered by about 6 inches of water he lies head down at an angle of about 30° with his tail occasionally breaking the surface. I had a non-taking fish in this lie for a while which was most annoying, preventing possible taking fish from moving in. He was a fish easily recognised by a scar on the top leading edge of his tail. He remained in the lie in front of the rock for three days head down and his tail waving gently in disdain at all my offerings. Fortunately a hint of rain moved him on before I was driven to carrying out the threats I was muttering against his person.

One day, I was watching the fish running the falls on a spate. This particular day there was a continous stream of grilse and salmon taking the falls. The ones that got it right first time avoided the white water and went up the solid water, just showing the odd squirt as they went up and over. Others that didn't get it right would lose their grip in the white water, lose momentum and balance, and the force of the water would dash them into the pool. Sitting at the top, I picked out a small fish lying tight into the rock face at the side of the fall and about 3 ft. up the fall.

It was in a little pocket of solid water formed by a vertical protrusion of rock jutting out about an inch, he had his nose pressed tight up to it. I watched him for a couple of minutes. He suddenly shot out into the main current, only made a couple of feet vertically, got caught by the white water and was thrown back into the pool. I was feeling rather sorry for the little chap, when suddenly there he was back with his nose pressed into the same crack, a brief pause, and off he shot, this time at a different angle, and vanished, only to appear tucked into the rock side halfway up the fall where there is an eddy that's used as a stage post by quite a few fish. A short rest, and off he shot again, and got it all wrong and was thrown back into the pool. I watched the protrusion and after a few minutes, there he was, another pause, and up and into the eddy, paused for a moment and he was off again. I saw a slight flick of water at the top of the fall, and he was gone.

From what I have observed since, I'm quite certain that salmon have, for want of a better way of describing it, a learning curve.

As I've said, the falls present quite a fearsome obstacle to the fish. When there is a good spate, the fish negotiate it in a steady stream. When the spate coincides with the grilse run, even though the falls are 30 miles from the sea, the fish are up and over, and on another 8 miles into the loch still with sea lice on them.

The cream of my salmon fishing is a fresh run grilse covered in sea lice on a Yellow Dolly—marvellous.

It is very interesting comparing dry fly for salmon in summer, which is a visual form of fishing, to the blind faith of spring fishing with a 4″ fly in February and March. They are at the extreme ends of salmon fishing. Light and on the top. Heavy and on the bottom.

Both methods have their fascination, and I cannot put one in front of the other. Whether it's the sudden rise of a salmon to a greased Yellow Dolly on a summer's day, or the tug of a huge spring fish on a sunken line after many freezing days of blind faith. They are both electrifying and are the reasons that all paths lead to the river.

I fished the Helmsdale one day, and was very keen to try the Yellow Dolly. I took Albert, the head stalker, with me. I had a rod for the week, but only time to spare for a couple of days fishing. He would fish the other days and also have a crack at the sea trout at night. On the Helmsdale, you must take one of the river ghillies. This was fine, our man was a keeper from a neighbouring estate, so there was a lot of local chat. The problem was knowing precisely where the fish were lying. The ghillie's instructions were to start here and finish there. I fished using a Badger Tube, just fishing the water in the conventional way, keeping an eye open for anywhere that I could try a Yellow Dolly.

Fishing down a shady pool, a fish moved at the fly—a Yellow Dolly candidate?—I put the Badger back over him, and he took it. Albert sat watching, the ghillie straight away sprang to his feet for a net. Where was it? We hadn't brought one! Albert motioned him to sit tight. I played the fish and eventually, it rolled over and I brought it into the side in front of Albert, who got up, strolled forward, picked it up by the tail, looked at the ghillie, and said 'I'm the net'. We finished the day with three fish, one on a Yellow Dolly.

On my river, having now got the measure of a Yellow Dolly, I generally fish conventionally down river with a Badger Tube or something similar, and change to Yellow Dollies either for the return upstream or if a fish moved, but wouldn't take.

It has developed into a competition between greased line fishing and dry fly, with the emphasis on the greased line, mainly I think, to ensure that I don't make extravagant claims for the Yellow Dolly.

It doesn't succeed every time. One year an officer of the Irish Guards on a very short leave, came to stay for two days. One of the keenest and most capable fisherman I've ever fished with. He shot off just after daybreak to fish the river, and make the most of his day. I went down just before lunch and found him four miles down the river at the 'Crooked Pool', laying flat on his back, rod at side, snoring gently.

Walking quietly past him to the edge of the run, I pulled line from the reel. At the sound of the ratchet he was bolt upright and wide awake, product of SAS training, no doubt. Anyway, I fished the lie and nothing. He had fished more or less the whole of the river down without success. I asked if he had fished the little pool further upstream which is tucked away in a bend of the river, and he said 'No'. 'Come on', I said, 'we will try it, if we can't catch one there, we may as well go trout fishing on the loch'. He refused to fish the pool, insisting that I show him how this little fly of mine was fished. I put on a Yellow Dolly and fished it upstream. At the lie, I rose, hooked, and lost a fish. He still could not be persuaded to fish, but insisted that I should try again for the other fish I said could be in the lie. I did, and couldn't move a fish, despite going down in size. 'Now you must try a "Wiggler" on him, and wipe my eye', I told him. This he could not resist. He tied on a 'Wiggler', covered the lie, up came the fish, and he wiped my eye. A 'Wiggler' is a fly that he ties on a small Esmond Drury hook, and consists of about ten strands of Deer Hair, and three strands of Peacock herl which extend twice the length of the hook beyond the tail. The head is finished with a couple of turns of yellow, blue or orange hackle.

I tie a similar fly with a few strands of badger hair, dyed yellow on aluminium tubes or low water doubles and finished with a yellow or orange hackle.

If you ever want to win favour with your wife, daughter or girlfriend, persuade her to part with a lock of hair. Tie a very

PLATE 11

A stealthy fisherman sees many things

The Canadian tagging system illustrated on a Scottish salmon. See page 102

PLATE 12

Canada – Steven Wilson, my guide on the Miramichi

Setting out in canoes, each visitor with his own guide

small pinch on one side of a half inch aluminium tube, so the the hair protrudes slightly more than an inch beyond the end of the tube, finish with two turns of yellow hackle tied flat. The colour of hair does not matter, as long as it is no more than a couple of dozen strands to give movement. It is as good as any fly, and better than most.

On another occasion I had a fanatical sea trout fishing friend to stay, who was a very good salmon fisherman. He used a little calculator, which, from the input of temperature, height of water, month of the year, and no doubt a great deal of experience, told him the size of fly. His chosen pattern was a blue and black tube about an inch overall. I had sent him off down the river in the morning, and said that I would come down later and meet up with him just after lunch. This I did, he had fished three pools without any success. The river was in good order so I told him not to worry, the next pool would produce a fish. When we got there, I instructed him where he should start and that there was only one good taking lie and once he had covered it, he could stop fishing and we would go on to another pool. He fished it down, covered the lie, and a fish took him, which he played and eventually landed. He suggested I should fish it down, which I did, with a Yellow Dolly and took a fish from the same lie. We fished this pool all afternoon, resting the pool between fish. He caught three fish on his blue and black tube and I followed him down each time with a Yellow Dolly and caught three fish. We had six fish for the day and called it quits. I'm certain we could have caught them with any fly of the right size. It does illustrate how running fish drop into a lie for a brief rest and a breather. As quickly as we created a vacancy another fish took over.

A good gillie knows all such lies on his beat and its this knowledge that catches the fish for the rod and makes his engagement well worth while.

Sitting by the river as I've said before is one of my favourite ways of 'fishing'. I was doing this one day by the side of the Rede in Northumberland a few yards from the edge of the river in a little glade amongst the riverside trees. I was sitting facing the pool elbows on knees trying to thread the nylon leader through the tiny eye of a snipe and purple. A stoat came running along the bank, under my leg and stopped between my legs rose up on its haunches and looked me straight in the eye, the expression 'Oh! Hell' flashed across his face and he jumped straight into the river and swam at great speed to the other side, where he hunted along the bank as though nothing had happened.

What has that to do with fishing? You may ask. Nothing! Other than I was sat in exactly the same spot on another occasion doing exactly the same thing when I heard a splash, looked up and saw a swirl a couple of yards out from the bank.

A big trout I thought and continued tying on my trout flies. Again another splash, a lot more solid this time. That's not a trout. Too heavy a sound, its more like a salmon. It was near the end of May so it could be a salmon. What could I do? I was only four yards from the fish, I could crawl away and fish down to him from further upstream as there was no chance of an approach from below. I decided to stay put, the fish could not have seen me or he would not have risen. I slowly tied on a new 6 lb. leader and a Yellow Dolly, greased them and pulled enough line out of the rod tip to flick the fly a yard beyond and upstream of the rise. I lifted the little trout rod to draw the fly over the lie. The salmon's head came out of the water by the fly, he did not take it. I flicked it back, again his head came out and the fly disappeared. I lifted the rod and he was on. I stood up, the fish took off across the pool, jumped, landed on the rocks at the far side fell back in to the river and then bored and jumped again. I bent the little trout rod into him and he calmed down and I got him under control. Eventually I popped him head first into the trout net all 12½ lbs. and dragged him ashore. Before you say it, I use a net when trout fishing!

8

Canada

In the spring of 1985 I was preparing my book when on holiday in Portugal. On the flight home I was thinking about what I had written, when I had a brainwave—some would say a brainstorm. If La Branche could come over to Scotland to try his method, then surely I should go to Canada and try mine. What a good idea, particularly as I couldn't do any worse than La Branche. If it didn't work in Canada, so what, I would at least see how they went about catching salmon, and possibly see the reason for failure, if I failed.

Immediately I got home, I wrote to the Wildlife Resources Department of New Brunswick, and to the Miramichi Salmon Association for any information they could give me. They both responded promptly with lots of literature. The Secretary of the Miramichi Salmon Association, Mrs. Wilma Spencer of Boiestown, sent a list of outfitters to choose from. I stuck a pin in her list and came up with the Wilson Fishing Camps, Macnamee, New Brunswick. I rang them, spoke to Keith Wilson, who sounded very nice on the telephone. I explained that I wanted to catch an Atlantic Salmon on a dry fly. He was not certain about catching a salmon on a dry fly, but I would have every opportunity of catching a fish.

The pin had made the decision, and I liked Mr. Wilson's frankness, so I booked for the only week I was free to go—the 20th–27th July.

I arranged all the flights and advance bookings, marked the dates in my diary, and then put it out of my mind. There were seven weeks before departure, and I had many other things to do.

A day or two before departure, I got out the tickets and other literature, and ran through travel times and the other information I had been sent from Canada. There looking at me was a statement 'Treble hooks not allowed, only flies tied on single or double hooks permitted'. Oh dear, my Yellow Dollies were illegal.

I dashed to the fly tying kit and proceeded to tie a Yellow Dolly version on the small doubles I use for Sea Trout flies. I tied a bunch of yellow hair on top of the hook to make half the skirt, doubled the hair back under the shank, and whipped it down. This method gave an acceptable skirt, and the red tying silk over the hair made the bodice. A shawl of black hair and the fly looked fine. Off to the river to try it. I cast across the current, and as it came round it sank, the weight of the double hook was too much and I couldn't bring it back on to the top of the water.

Back to the fly tying kit—this time a variety of single hooks. Wilson Low Water size 10, various trout hooks in sizes 8 to 16.

The small hooks size 14 to 16 with the new tying fished the rough water very well. I hastily tied up a selection of these as my Canadian Yellow Dollies, also a few Yellow Badgers on low water doubles, size 10 and 12. I put them along with a few trout flies into a plastic fly box. I decided to take two fly rods, not really knowing what I might be faced with; my 14 foot, 3 piece, double handed rod and my 9 foot, 2 piece, which fitted nicely into the same bag as the long rod. Both reels with floating lines, a tin of mucilin, a reel of 8 lb. nylon, polarised glasses, thermometer and my waders made up the rest of the kit.

I set off from Newcastle via Heathrow to Halifax in Nova Scotia. The Atlantic crossing in a Boeing 767 took $6\frac{1}{2}$ hours, and passed very quickly. I had to stay overnight in Halifax before travelling on to Fredrickton in New Brunswick the following morning.

Halifax was like most other cities, with modern highrise buildings in the centre. On the outskirts, there were some very nice wooden houses, and lots of open spaces.

I went walking through the common, and was pleasantly surprised to see elms and horsechestnut trees, and the same grasses and weeds that grow in England. There were many young people playing baseball, tennis and cricket—joggers and runners, and lots of people walking, all enjoying the sunshine, and a temperature of 70° in the shade. It was so warm walking I had to take off my cap and carry my jacket.

The itinerary from Wilsons Camps said that noon 'til 4.00 p.m. was siesta time. I was now beginning to realise that it was going to be quite warm in the middle of the day, and my choice of fishing clothes could have been better.

I wandered around to overcome the 4 hours time change, not going to bed until 11.00 p.m., the equivalent of 3.0' clock in the morning in England.

Frederickton at last. After an uneventful flight from Halifax via Monckton, landing at 12.20, on time. I looked for Keith Wilson, and couldn't see anyone that matched the voice on the 'phone'. Then a neat grey haired lady caught my eye, and I had a premonition that she was the person I should meet. I walked towards her, she looked at me and said 'Mr. Knowles? I'm Keith's mother, I've been sent because everyone else is busy'. It was easy for her to recognize me, I was the only passenger with a fishing rod.

I loaded everything into the big estate car, and we were off on the road to Macnamee and the Wilson Sporting Camp. Grandma Wilson was a charming, quietly spoken lady and described all the places we passed through, and answered all my questions, and asked as many herself, about England and Scotland.

When we arrived, she took me into the office, I signed the

visitors book, she then told me that all the well known Scottish flies had gone out of favour, and the guides wouldn't use them, and produced a board of the current favourites. What a shock, I had never seen anything like them before. Fat hairy caterpillars, up to two inches long with $\frac{1}{2}$ inch thick bodies of spun deer hair in white and brown. The current favourite for warm water was nearly an inch long with a $\frac{1}{4}''$ thick body made of spun deer hair of hideous bright sickly green colour. Recovering from the shock, I could only say 'I don't know what Albert will say when he sees these beasties'.

I had the thought that, if nothing else came of this trip, a photograph of 4 or 5 of them would show that salmon will take anything at times.

A quick lunch in the kitchen, the main lunch was over, then I went for a walk, eager to look at the Miramichi before the resident fishermen arose from their lunchtime siesta. The second shock arrived. The South West Miramichi, 60 miles from the sea, was bigger than the Tay at Dunkeld. A better description might be three Aberdeenshire Dees, where the Miramichi split into three channels with the same clear gravel bedded waters as the Dee. Thoughts of putting a Yellow Dolly on the nose of a fish in such a huge river receded fast. The advantage was definitely with La Branche. I didn't feel optimistic.

Back at the camp, I met Keith Wilson, who had the easy manner of his mother. He was responsible for organising the fishing and the guides, and he briefly described, with an infectious enthusiasm, what the programme might be. Yes, the Miramichi was big, but it would fall a little during the week, and I would get a crack at the salmon with a dry fly, and possibly have an afternoon on a tributary of the Miramichi.

Sitting having supper in the Lodge on my own, the other fishermen were fishing, I thought to myself 'The pin in the map had led me to this spot in Canada, and I'm going to have a very,

very interesting week'.

The morning came as daylight filtered into my little wooden cabin at 5.30 a.m. I looked out of the window, the mist was forming, where the Miramichi, hidden by trees, wended its course. A quick stroll along the road looking at the neat wooden houses, not a dozen altogether, that make up the village of Macnamee. Then, after a good substantial breakfast, I was ready to meet the day.

Steven Wilson was to be my guide. 30 years old, fourth generation of Wilsons at Macnamee. The camp had been created by his great grandfather and had been run by the family every since.

Steven had fished the Miramichi from a boy, and had been a class 1 guide for 12 years, and it was soon evident that he knew his job.

We were all transported to the river. Five guides and five anglers to fish the morning session from 8 a.m. to 12 a.m. In accordance with the State laws each visiting angler fishing from a canoe must be accompanied by a class 1 guide, who can fish with the angler's rod if so requested by the angler.

Steven and I were fishing the lower of the camp's three beats. Rod, fishing bag etc. were loaded into our 20 foot wooden canoe, which had a little camping arm chair in the bows for the fisherman to take his ease and could be taken from the canoe and put on the beach to sit in.

We pushed off, and I sat watching the scene develop in front of me. It was magical, being transported in a canoe down a big powerful Canadian river, surrounded by forests and wooded islands, gliding easily and effortlessly. It's a marvellous sensation, and the two miles we went downstream passed far too quickly. In the deep water the guides sat and paddled the canoe, but they preferred to stand in the stern and propel the canoe with a long pole. They are skilled watermen, and can lower a canoe gently down the rapids and punt up the side of the rough water.

Back to reality. We dropped anchor in about 5 inches of water, alongside a little gravel bar, to fish the head of a very wide run created by a large island splitting the river.

Steven informed me that the fish held right in the head of the run in two or three pockets in the gravel. I fished where I was told, and with the flies he put on, without success. We then waded forward so that he could point out the pockets, in the gravel, which had a powerful flow of water over them. They were ideal resting lies for a travelling fish. We then canoed further down river, along one of the many channels to where the water formed a powerful run about 50 yards wide. We were to spend the rest of the morning on this run, fishing from the bank, and by dropping down in the canoe.

The river temperature was 66°. I took off the local fly called The Green Machine, the name of the horrific beasty I had seen in the office, and put on one of my low water double hooked size 10 Yellow Badgers. Half way down the run, fishing from the canoe, a fish pulled, and I lifted the rod into a $3\frac{1}{2}$ lb. grilse.

I played the fish from the canoe for a while, then Steven beached the canoe, and I continued from the bank. The fish was a determined little chap, fighting and leaping right out of the water until eventually Steven slipped the net under him.

He killed the fish, released the fly and then put his knife through the wrist of the tail just over the backbone and tagged it with one of my five New Brunswick fishing tags. He said that if he was found with a fish on the bank, or anywhere else, without a tag in it, he would lose his licence. No excuses. The Wildlife Rangers patrol the rivers in the manner of our Bailiffs. They accept no excuses, and can fine, impound and arrest on the spot. Everyone knows precisely what will happen if they break the fishing laws.

I gave the fish to Steven. I couldn't take it to England, and he hadn't had a fresh run salmon for himself that season. In fact, as he revealed later, he had never been given a fish in his 12 years as a guide.

The lunchtime transport arrived at midday, and I was told that we would start the evening session at 4.00 p.m. and fish until 9.00 p.m., and we would spend the whole of the session fishing the run we were just leaving.

A quick wash and change and then a very good Canadian lunch or dinner, the midday meal is the main meal of the day, after which I retired to my little cabin in the trees, stretched out on my bed, the midday heat is tremendous, and passed quickly into the land of Nod.

4.00 p.m. and we were off to continue where we had left off at lunchtime.

Starting again, I fished the run down with a Yellow Badger from the canoe, and moved a fish. I put up a Yellow Dolly that I had tied on a size 14 single hook, but couldn't move the fish, or with a size 16 that I clipped down to $\frac{3}{8}''$ in length. I re-fished the run from the bank, and a fish moved to the Yellow Dolly near the bottom of the run. The fish wouldn't move again to the Yellow Dolly.

The barbecue supper was ready, so we had a break for half an hour. During supper, Steven said he wouldn't start with dry flies until the water got a lot warmer. So I decided to try a size 10 Yellow Badger, even though the temperature had risen to 70°. I fished it down and went seven or eight yards further and got a good solid take from a fresh run salmon of about 10 lbs. He put up a tremendous fight, did two beautiful leaps, and ran me to the last five yards of backing twice before we netted him.

I unhooked him, and put him back, holding him gently for a half a minute in the current. All salmon as opposed to grilse must be returned to the river unharmed, this is part of the Canadian Government's effort to improve their salmon rivers. A few large bubbles of air came out of his gills, and he swam off into the deep. So ended a very interesting day, which I had throughly enjoyed, and left me with a lot to think about.

Next morning, much to my surprise, we returned to the same pool along with two American guests and their guides. I was to fish from the right bank with a downstream wind, and the Americans from the Island which formed the opposite bank. The water temperature had fallen overnight to 68° so I started with the No. 10 Yellow Badger, and fished the pool all the way down, hoping to move a fish so that I could try to catch it with a Yellow Dolly. At the tail of the run, some two yards lower down, where I took the salmon the night before, I felt a fish pull, lifted the rod, and I was into a fish.

The warm water brings out the best in the fish, and he fought like a tiger, running me on to the backing and making some really spectacular leaps. When he was netted, he was a grilse of about $4\frac{1}{2}$ lbs.

We were allowed to keep him, but he had fought so well, we gave him the thumbs up and put him back.

I had to stay in this pool called Stanley Lyon until midday. I fished it down twice and moved two fish to a Yellow Dolly, and two fish to a Yellow Badger, but none of them made a second offer.

I gave Steven the rod, and went for a stroll along the bank. Returning, I sat on a rock and watched him fishing. His style was similar to mine, shooting a lot of line but using slightly more line on his back cast, and more power with a little double haul motion to shoot a good length of line on his forward cast.

He let the current fish the fly, and didn't fish the fly by stripping line. After he had fished the run, we sat and chattered about fishing in general, and then I gave it another quick run down, hooked a fish half way down on the Badger, felt the weight, and he was gone.

Lunchtime, Keith Wilson picked us up and drove the party

back to camp. He asked if I would like Steven to take me to Cairns river to try for a sea going brook trout. I accepted. It was an opportunity to see another river and have the afternoon off from salmon fishing.

At 4.00 p.m. Steven and I set off for a tremendous day in the backwoods, 15 miles of dirt road, single track, and very rough in places; arriving finally at a beautiful clearing with a log cabin and a marvellous view of the river. It sparkled in the sunshine and had a backcloth of primeval woodland. The water appeared dark and peat stained from a distance. It was actually as clear as crystal, the dark stones in the river bed gave it the dark peaty look.

We whiled away a little time, Steven made an early supper, which we ate on the verandah of the cabin in the sunshine soaking up the sun and the scenery. He wanted to go downstream about two miles, to a pool that he was fairly certain would hold a fish, but he didn't want to get there until the sun was off the water.

About 6.00 p.m. we set off wading downstream, following the banks, crossing and recrossing on the gravel bars, to avoid the deeper side of the pools.

The forest was impenetrable, and the bed of the river was the only way to travel. It brought to mind Indians and trappers and the settlers that first arrived in New Brunswick. The going wasn't easy in waders and carrying a fishing rod. It must have been terribly difficult for the first settlers carrying everything they required to sustain life.

Signs of animals were evident in the mud along the banks and bars. Moose, white tail deer and beaver predominated. Empty fresh water mussel shells were scattered in the shallows and on the river banks. I asked Steven if they ate fresh water mussels or fished them for pearls. He said that you could eat them if they were boiled for a long time, but no one did, and they didn't find pearls in them. The Racoons loved them, and fished for them leaving the shells scattered along the gravel bars. We saw a big owl with a wing span of around four feet, which Steven called a cat owl.

We finally arrived at the selected fishing spot. Luckily we were still dry, the water at one crossing point came within an inch of the top of my waders.

I was to wade very slowly out to a point nearly half way across the river and make a long cast across the slow deep tail of the pool with a white moth-like dry fly. Steven was a little apprehensive. The lie was alongside a shelf of rock forming the far bank that dropped off into a deep channel, which he said had a flat rock bottom about ten feet long, with a boulder in the middle. This was the lie that we had journeyed two miles downstream for, and the gamble that a good fish was in residence.

A very intriguing situation. A slow stealthy stalk, then floating the line away downstream to make one extremely long cast. It isn't very often you make such an effort, and the result depends on just one cast.

Not at home. The monster sea-going brook trout was on vacation. Poor Steven, he was disappointed. 'Never mind', I said, 'I wouldn't have missed the chance for anything'.

We caught a few small brook trout, which we released.

The journey back was broken by a few casts in odd pools. Coming round one bend in the river, we saw a white tailed deer feeding on water weed in the shallows. She put her head into about ten inches of water, which came over her eyes, and pulled out great strands of water weed that hung like a goatee beard as she chewed away.

I watched her with the binoculars for a couple of minutes. She was about the weight of an average red deer hind. We moved on a few steps, the deer saw the movement, and in great leaps, crossed the river with white tail flared upright. She gave one huge bound, out of the river and vanished into the trees.

The mosquitoes arrived with the dusk. Hasty applications of repellant kept the majority at bay, but a few penetrated.

The camp appeared in the last of the evening light. We went upstream a little way above the camp to a small pool above a gravel bar. Ideal. The fading light of the evening sky reflected on the pool, and there was a gentle upstream wind. I said to Steven how perfect it was, even I would be able to see the fish take the fly. A little black object appeared swimming from the dark of the bank and crossed the middle of the pool. Suddenly, there was a great flurry in the water, and 'thwack', the Beaver's tail struck the water. A short swim under water and its head appeared to be joined by another, and they swam upstream. What a way to end our night's fishing.

Fishless we might be, but certainly one of the finest nights I've ever spent on a river, and we had fire flies flickering along the river bank as we returned to the cabin.

Wednesday morning, 8.00 a.m. the two Americans and I went to the top beat and fished all the way down the beat from the canoes without seeing a fish. It's a marvellous way to fish in a canoe drifting gently through the pools, dropping anchor upstream of a lie or run, and fishing over it. Then drifting through to see if there are any fish.

La Branche's description of drifting down through pools counting fish, and then going back upstream to fish for them made a lot more sense now I had experienced it.

The transport was waiting for us at the bottom of the beat and took the party back to camp for lunch. I was now firmly attached to the two Americans and their guides.

We were operating from three canoes drifting down river, fishing off gravel bars, or dropping anchor and fishing the runs from the canoes.

We dined at the same table, and kept up a constant chatter about the ways of England, Scotland and the Americas.

We took a trip to Doakstown in the afternoon to Wallace W. Doak, the local fishing tackle shop to buy a few of the local flies— Bradfords, Buck Bugs, Green Machines and Bombers.

The evening session continued from where we had left the canoes. We split up immediately, each going down one of the many different runs created by long islands splitting the river into three or four channels, each a good size river in itself. The Miramichi is certainly a huge river, and must be awesome in the spring breakup, with the melting snow and the ice breaking on the river, the whole lot raging down in a huge flood. The marks on the trees showed that it must come down as a great mass of water and ice. In the spring after the breakup, the season opens with the Black Salmon fishing, which we know as kelts. This spring fishing was carried out by the Indians and settlers as a source of food after the hard winter. It is still carried on today as a sport. The Wilson's Camps have fishermen who come year after year specially for the Black Salmon fishing.

We arrived at the 'Home pool' for supper, where the last two hours were to be spent. The 'Home pool' is a long rough run of water along a very high wooded bank, with a few big boulders for lies. One American waded from the gravel island, the other fished from the bank, and I fished from the canoe. My guide didn't think we would have much chance of an offer. We could only fish a series of drops down the far side of the main run without interfering with the Americans. It was better water for the Yellow Dolly, and I fished it for 2 'drops', as the guide called each move. He then suggested the Green Machine, which produced nothing. Another change to a Bradford as we finished the fourth drop. I said to the guide that I would go back to the Yellow Dolly after the next cast, and re-fish the drop. The line went tight and I was into a grilse of about 4 lbs., and what a fighter.

He leapt at least twelve times, high out of the water, and would not come to the boat. The Canadian salmon, pound for pound, are far more powerful than similar fish at home. They have tremendous energy, and will not give in. Steven finally decided to beach the canoe and the fish was netted from the shore by him after some desperate stabs with the net. The only fish caught, and I had missed another opportunity to cover a taking fish with the Yelow Dolly.

Next morning, we all returned to the 'Home Pool'. The Americans taking up their previous night's position, and two new American guests fishing from the shore. With all the run taken up by the Americans, Steven took me in the canoe to fish 'drops'. This time I decided to fish with the Yellow Dolly, and I fished it through the four drops, to no avail. Crossing the tail of the run, we landed, and I fished the bottom half of the run from the shore. The American fishing from the shore upstream of me, got into his canoe and moved over to join his friend on the island.

My guide suggested moving up and trying a Badger. I had not seen any fish move during the hour and a half we had fished the run, so I put on the Yellow Badger. A quarter of the way down, and a fish surged at the fly, and he was on, a lovely little grilse that I beached while Steven took some cine film with my camera. Again I had missed the opportunity of taking a fish. On went the Yellow Dolly, and I fished it down, and at very nearly the same spot, a fish surged at the Yellow Dolly, but I never touched it when I lifted the rod. I gave it a few more casts, nothing moved. I changed, went smaller, cast at the lie,the fly came round and I fully expected the fish to take. Nothing moved. A few more casts, then I went to an in-between size, still no offer. I thought that if he wouldn't take a Yellow Dolly, then I should try a Badger, and get an eye wipe.

Both sizes of Badger, 10s and 12s went over the lie, nothing moved, the fish had gone on.

The remainder of the morning session was blank for fish and rises.

In the afternoon we canoed downstream from the Home Pool, stopping at different pools and lies. I had supper on one of the islands, and then on to the Stanley Lyon Pool, arriving at 8.00 p.m.

The three of us concentrated on the pool for what I was now accepting to be the best part of the day. Not a fish moved, and I had the feeling that the water had dropped away too much for the pool to hold fish even briefly.

Friday dawned, the Americans last day. We all went to the top beat and proceeded downstream, taking different channels. It was a beautiful day, and our progress down a tree lined channel was lovely. Sat in the little folding camping chair in the bow of the canoe, we glided down runs and floated along slacker currents, looking for fish. Stopping occasionally to fish a known lie, then drifting over it looking through polarised glasses to see if we had fished over any fish. We didn't see any fish all the way down the beat, though that didn't matter, it's such a splendid relaxed way to fish. An osprey came over us, hunting his way up the river. He had a few plunging dives into the river, which produced a similar result to ours.

The evening session was to be the climax of the Americans' week. Both were fishless, but eager to fish the 'Home Pool' which was to be ours for the whole of the evening session.

We fished from 4.30 for two hours without a sign of a fish, then stopped early for supper.

On the island at the head of the main run there is a picnic table. The guides made a fire and cooked sausages. Gathered around the table, Jim and John, my two American companions, chattered about the week and its highlights. Whiling away the time hoping a fish might show as the sun went off the water. I offered Jim the use of a Yellow Badger for his last hours of fishing. This he hastily accepted. He had never caught a salmon, and the Yellow Badger had gained a reputation for catching fish.

PLATE 13

SOME SALMON LURES USED IN CANADA

Brown Bomber

Rat-faced McDougall

Author's Yellow Badger

Buck Bug, red and
green butt

White Wulff

Green Brolly made after
Canada

Enlarged photograph showing a Bradford, Yellow Dolly on a single hook and a
Yellow Badger

PLATE 14

Green Brolly and Yellow Badger
Three Bombers
Buck Bug, Yellow Dolly, $\frac{1}{4}$" Badger Tube, Yellow Dolly, Single hook Yellow Dolly

Canadian Dry Flies
Two Bombers (1985)
Colonel Monell (1924)

Colonel Monell
Author's tying

At 7.30, Jim and John, took up station on the island side of the main run. There was a blustery downstream wind. I, being left-handed, crossed in the canoe to fish from the bank. I sat there watching the water. Not a fish showed, and I was quite happy to sit and watch Jim and John fishing.

A sudden cry from John, and a grilse leapt high in the air and was gone. Fish were beginning to move. Then Jim let out a great shout of triumph. He was hooked into a salmon. John kept on fishing. I sat content to watch Jim play his fish. He was in a state of great excitement giving a hilarious commentary to his guide and the world in general, in the way only Americans can in their drawling twang.

John hooked another grilse, and this one stayed on. Fortunately, Jim's fish had fought away downstream. His guide had launched the canoe and with Jim aboard had followed it. They were now on the other side of the second run. The fish had been on for half an hour, and they didn't appear to be tiring the fish.

John's fish was way down the main run with about a hundred yards of backing. He was rooted to the spot where he was standing when he hooked the fish. I shouted to him to follow the fish. He shouted back that he still had lots of backing left on his reel, and remained firmly rooted to the spot. Eventually they both landed their fish at the same time—9.00 p.m. Jim having taken 45 minutes to better his fish. Great shouts of triumph, overjoyed with success. Jim's at 12 lbs. was returned. John's a 4 lb. grilse was tapped on the head and tagged. What a marvellous way to end their week's fishing. A long hard week of flogging the water, and to achieve success in the last moments of their fishing vacation. Jim's fish was his first salmon ever, and he was absolutely on cloud nine, and returning the fish had given him tremendous pleasure. 'Gee', he said, 'You should have seen him swim away'.

What a marvellous attitude, it gave me a great feeling to have helped this wonderful American to catch his fish. His occupation is teaching handicapped children. A fine man.

The next day, Saturday, was my last, and I would be fishing the Home Pool, both morning and evening.

I concentrated on the Yellow Dolly, and used the largest I had, and fished the run down. Nothing moved. Two local anglers fished the island side down without any success. We changed sides and I went down the outside of the run in the canoe in three drops.

Fishing the last drop, I saw a flash in the water, just out of casting distance. A few moments later the angler on the bank shouted that a salmon had shown between him and our canoe. Steven promptly decided the fish I'd seen was moving up the run, so he poled back and dropped me on the island, telling me to fish down to the lie in midstream. Too late, the angler on the bank hooked the fish and landed a 10 lb. salmon. It proved how quickly Steven read the situation, and how swiftly the fish moved up the run. No other fish moved, and we retired for lunch.

The evening session saw four of us going out to concentrate on the Home Pool. This, I thought, was rather over-doing things, so I landed on the island. The temperature of the water had risen from 68° in the morning to 74°, and I decided to sit and watch the others fish, and wait for the sun to go off the water. It was very pleasant in the evening sunshine. The forest climbing high up from the edge of the river a multicolour of browns and greens. The golden light of the evening sun highlighting the scene making sparkling lights on the water. Bees humming, flies flitting and darting, the flash of a fly line as it looped in a cast, the heron like fishermen blending into this picture of serene bliss. Steven lit a fire and brewed tea, then barbequed some beef burgers. We sat at the table watching the anglers fishing and chatting to the new arrival, an American, and like all the anglers I'd seen during the week, he fished with a nine foot rod. He was the first one I'd seen double haul with so much power, and he cast a very good long line. He waded in sneakers, just wading into the river, further than most other fishermen wearing chest waders.

Chatting to him at supper he said that his rod was rated at AFTM 8, and he double hauled salt water fishing for bass with a fly. He said that he was occasionally bitten by leeches when wading in the rivers but he now stayed out of the stiller water.

The sun finally went off the water at 8.00 p.m., and I reckoned that I could fish the run down three times by wading downstream from the Island. This would let me use both sizes of Yellow Dolly, and finish with a Yellow Badger.

My success or failure was now down to the final 60 minutes. It was not to be; like La Branche in Scotland, I failed in Canada. What a marvellous experience though. I had learned a lot, met some really nice people, and had many new experiences.

The night on Cairns river I shall always remember.

The Miramichi River, so very big and so beautiful in its tree lined setting with its many channels and islands.

The guides, and particularly Steven Wilson, his skill with a canoe, and infinite knowledge of the river. Every boulder, every pothole in the gravel bars, he knew like the back of his hand. It is this intimate knowledge that makes a ghillie well worth his fee when fishing on strange waters.

Chatting to the guides, I said that I'd learned a lot from them, and thanked them for their generosity and knowledge.

They were keen for me to send them a Yellow Badger, and Steven wanted a Yellow Dolly, which he was convinced would catch salmon even though it had not produced a fish.

I am quite certain that the fly would catch Miramichi salmon. I tackled the fish with the same technique as I use in Scotland, locating the fish with an ordinary fly, then using the dry fly.

I'm afraid I took too long to appreciate that the fish were running through a lot quicker than I realised, and they never remained in any lie for more than a few minutes. That's why the

change of fly hardly produced a rise. It was interesting to be told
that the technique in low water and high temperatures, when
fish were holed up in cool water pools, was to fish a 2″ long dry
fly called a Bomber. This big hairy caterpillar-like fly is cast
upstream and allowed to float freely downstream, past the fisherman, and then drag with a wake as the current catches the fly.
Salmon rise and attempt to drown it revealing their lie. The angler
can then concentrate on the fish. This must be in low water, when
the fish stop running. There is a great similarity between their
technique and mine.

The Canadian dry fly fisherman has moved on from the big
Palmer hackled flies of La Branche to Bombers tied on long shank
single hooks and Buck Bugs which have spun deer hair bodies
and are greased to give flotation. Also the Wulff series of Dry
flies and the many variations like the Rat Faced McDougall are
extremely popular.

The blurb in a fishing tackle catalogue says 'Dry Fly Fishing
is becoming more popular every year and with good reason. Dry
flies especially the Bomber tend to arouse the curiosity of even
the laziest fish, and although they don't necessarily catch more
they do liven up the action'. It goes on to describe the Buck Bug
'This is unquestionably the best selling fly in our showcases.
Nobody seems to know exactly why it works but few will argue
with its results. While some prefer to use it as a dry fly, the vast
majority of anglers fish it wet. Either way it catches fish, and,
after all, that is the whole point'.

The Buck Bug reads like the ideal fly for the sceptics in this
country, fish it wet and if it fails grease it and fish it dry.

The Canadians have a preference for short rods, nine or ten
feet long and the guides were very amused when I produced my
fourteen foot rod, 'Gee, are you going to poke his eye out' was
one comment. They had never seen a long rod used on their river
and were impressed with the ease a long line could be cast. All

of them are good fisherman and within minutes they mastered the double handed style. None were converted. All their fishing techniques have developed from the use of short rods. Dibbling as practiced in the North of Scotland requires a long rod to dibble the dropper across the current. The Canadian equivalent is a hitch over the eye of the fly which prevents the fly from fishing true and skitters it across the surface. They also use flies with protruding tufts of hair which when greased and stripped across the surface bounce and tumble like a dibbled fly.

If the Canadians had had a spring run of fish that required large flies and sinking lines as in this country then they would have had a need for long powerful rods. As it is they get along quite nicely with their nine and ten foot rods though the universal use of canoes does reduce the need to wade and cast great distances.

During the conversation with the guides and fishermen I met, it was apparent that dry fly fishing is not used by as many fishermen as I thought, and when they do use it it is as a last resort in hot weather when wet fly fails.

I had the impression before my trip, that the majority of salmon were caught on dry fly, they are not. All the fishermen I spoke to were conscious of dry fly, and some used it at times, all assured me that salmon did take a floating fly.

The majority of Canadian salmon are caught on wet fly fished with a floating line in exactly the same way as on this side of the Atlantic. The patterns used are different, though the sizes are the same, bearing in mind that their fish are adapted to higher temperatures.

Two of their flies which appealed to me are the Bradford with which I caught a fish, and the Butterfly. The Butterfly is the most popular fly used on the South West Miramichi.

The 'Bomber' with its spun deer hair body, thick and fat with a thinly palmered hackle was not compatible with my thoughts on dry fly, or sizes related to temperature.

The most notable difference between Canada and Scotland was the water temperature. The flies I used were operating at a temperature difference of about 10°. What I fish with in Scotland at 60° was right for the Miramichi at 70°. The Yellow Badger, even though it was the wrong fly for my purpose, proved to be the most effective fly used that week, and the Miramichi Atlantic Salmon were no different to Scottish fish as far as I could see.

Another striking thing was the power and stamina of the salmon, far superior to most Scottish salmon and this, I am certain, is due to the higher water temperatures giving them a more sustained release of energy.

Going there as I had direct from fresh summer fish in Scotland to fresh running fish in Canada the temperature difference was notable. My river temperatures the week before going to Canada, were from 56° to 62°, against 66° to 74° for the Miramichi. The difference in stamina caused by the 10 degree higher temperature was most striking. The Canadian fish took roughly twice as long to tire and bring to the net.

The finest thing of all was the sporting attitude of the American fishermen and the Canadian guides, and the enthusiasm everyone had for catch and release. They were determined that the salmon should regain its former glory. Their tagging system works in practice. The tags are put in the wrist of the tail by pushing a knife blade through the flesh just above the bone, passing the end of the tag through the hole, and locking it into the automatic clip. A system which should be introduced into the British Isles for all fishermen, including commercial netsmen, on and offshore.

The tags are numbered and entered on the permit (a better term than licence), and the fee paid before fishing. The use must be recorded immediately on the permit, and the tag inserted as soon as the fish is landed.

In Canada, the fee for anglers is approximately £10 per tag, limited to five tags for visiting anglers. The seasonal limit for resident anglers is ten.

Canada is different to the British Isles, in that some of the fishing is owned by the State, and some by private individuals.

In Britain it is nearly all in the hands of individuals.

This doesn't mean that tagging should not take place. The benefits are enormous, and for the first time ever, we would have a record of the annual catch by all means. The proceeds could be used, as in Canada, for ensuring the passage of fish and to improve the spawning beds in the head waters of the river systems. I think it is quite wrong that the on and offshore netsmen do not make any contribution towards the cost of producing smolts. The Greenlanders and Faroese do feed them. Our commercial fishermen make very little contribution to the production of salmon, and in real terms, have no right to them. If their fishing yields such a low return they cannot afford to pay £3 for a Salmon tag, then they should be bought out by the Government on economic grounds.

The Salmon is too valuable to the community as a sporting resource that generates tremendous revenue for rural economies, and gives pleasure to many people. If the present system continues, the salmon will decline, and the commercial netsmen are doomed along with the salmon.

It would be a shame to allow it to reach such a state before action is taken.

The statistics produced by New Brunswick, show that a rod-caught salmon is worth some £200 to the local economy, where as the commercial fish only generates £8.

Pressure needs to be brought to bear on our British Government by Tourist Boards, riparian owners (the value of their fishing is at stake), and sportsmen to keep their right to a leisure activity and to maintain the salmon for future generations.

9

Reflections and Experiments

The trip to Macnamee on the South West Miramichi in July 1985 was a wonderful experience. The sudden daft urge to catch a Canadian salmon on a dry fly had revealed a completely new scene. I had no idea what to expect when I set off, just a vision from Hewitt and La Branche of clear pools and salmon in ranks waiting for a dry fly. Reality was slightly different, the river was huge and clear. The fish were running, but I only saw one under water, and that was the flash of a running fish.

I canoed down many of the minor pools along the streams between the Islands, and despite much searching of the depths through polarized glasses, I never saw a fish, let alone one settled in a pool.

I could not have picked a better week for catching salmon. The river was falling in after a rise of water, slightly cloudy on the first day, and crystal clear for the rest of the week. A fair run of salmon and grilse went through the beats, all intent on the headwaters.

One offer from a fish and he was either caught or he continued on his way upstream. With hindsight, I should have perhaps been better 20 or 30 miles higher up the river.

However, that is after the event, and rather futile.

I experienced Canadian salmon fishing, and thoroughly enjoyed it. The people, the river, and the marvellous setting in natural forest, which, incidentally, made me realise that nearly every tree or woodland in the British Isles has been planted by man.

The fish were there, and I had my chance. I rose five fish with the Yellow Dolly, and two of them, I am quite certain, took the fly. I never touched one, and so like La Branche on his trip to Scotland, I on mine to Canada, failed.

Mulling it all over later, I realised that I had wasted a lot of time at the beginning of the week, when the main run of fish went through. I had been slow to appreciate that the rises I got were from briefly resting fish. Fishing to make them show with a Yellow Badger, only revealed a wasted opportunity. The fish were not lingering, and by the time I had changed the fly, they had moved on. That I could explain and put down to my slow-wittedness. It still left an uneasy feeling about two missed fish. The fact that I had been by far the most successful fisherman on the river was one up for the old country, but no real merit to me.

Before I left for Canada, I had experimented with Yellow Dollies tied on small trout doubles, which were too heavy and sank quickly in the rough water. At the last moment, I tied the Yellow Dollies on single hooks and went to Canada without trying them on fish. However, I was quite happy with the Yellow Dollies I had tied on size 14 and 16 single hooks.

The actual flies I used in Canada are shown in the photograph on Plate 13.

The flies fished extremely well in the rough water, and the fish acknowledged them by rising to them. Like La Branche 60 years ago, I was at a loss to explain why my flies, like his, didn't catch a fish.

Steven, my ghillie, filled the role of Arthur Wood, and like Wood, he could not offer any plausible reason for them not taking fish. Steven is an experienced guide, and well versed in dry fly fishing on the Miramichi. He was quite certain that the Yellow Dolly would catch fish, and was very taken by the fly. The way he fished a dry fly was to use a very large Bomber about 2″ long, cast it well upstream then let it float freely downstream until it was below him, and then draw it across the current creating a wake. This he said would fetch a fish up to the fly, though he got very few takes. Having found a fish, he then used a small Bomber of a Buck Bug to catch it.

He used a dry fly when the water got warmer, and when the fish had settled into cold water pools. These are pools with cold streams running in from the shade of the forest or the under water strata. He said that these lies in cooler water were very attractive to the fish during the very hot days of summer.

I thought it was very hot in July and was very relieved at not having to fish through the heat of the afternoon. My system is tuned to having a little siesta at lunchtime on the river bank at home, so I dropped quite naturally into their fishing routine.

Canadian salmon must be capable of withstanding water temperatures into the eighties. The guides said that the Miramichi had the hightest water temperature of all the rivers in Canada. I found it rather a puzzle that their fish responded to my low water flies and tiny Yellow Dollies at slightly higher temperatures than in Scotland, then to be told that at very high temperatures the fish responded to huge 'Bombers'. This went against all my ideas of size reduction linked to temperature increases. The temperature difference between Canadian and British salmon when linked to behaviour, was approximately 10 degrees. I know it is rather a bold statement to make after only six days fishing. I went to Canada direct from Scotland, where I had been fishing for fresh run grilse and salmon, and the flies and tactics I use in Scotland caught the fish in Canada. The only difference being the higher water temperature.

So the week had ended without a fish on the Yellow Dolly, but the whole trip had been well worthwhile. I had enjoyed it immensely, and learned a lot.

*   *   *   *   *   *   *   *   *   *

Back on my own river, which was still in good order, the fish were losing a little of their silver freshness, and getting a pink tinge; I went fishing with my Canadian Yellow Dollies. Would you believe it, in two days I rose twelve different salmon and never touched one of them.The twelfth fish was in the Rock Pool only twenty feet from me, and I had my glasses on. The fish rose, took the fly beautifully, turned down with it, I lifted the rod and never felt a thing!

Seventeen fish, and not one touched. I couldn't understand it. Was I losing my touch?

Shades of La Branche sixty years ago, when he fished on the Dee and rose many salmon with his Palmer tied dry flies. They took his flies down, and, in his words, did not close down on them, and he did not catch a fish. Here was I on my own river, faced with exactly the same problem.

Five fish in Canada, and twelve fish in Scotland, the majority of which I was certain had taken the fly properly. Arthur Wood had pulled La Branche's leg about it, saying that the fish had dislocated jaws and could not close down upon the fly. He then made the more serious suggestion that the stiff hackle tied on at right angles was preventing the hook from taking hold.

When I read Wood's description of the events that took place on the Dee, I had agreed with his stiff hackle theory, because when dapping, I have seen salmon and trout bounce a large Palmer tied dry fly like a football. A very large Palmer fly can bring trout up to the dap in a most spectacular way, crashing down on to the fly with the intention of drowning it. I now fish the dap using small Palmer flies and have a much more successful hooking rate when fishing for trout. All very interesting, and demonstrating that Scottish salmon do not get hooked on huge bushy dry flies. But my Canadian Yellow Dollies were tiny by comparison, so what was wrong. It could only be me, somehow reacting differently to the take of the fly, or the fly was at fault.

A whisky and a long soak in the bath resolved the problem—Go fishing with a proper Yellow Dolly and a tiny treble hook.

Next morning, I made a beeline for the nearest pool, with a suitable lie—Lower Allta Fearn, a pool with a rough streamy head which turns quickly in to a wide rippling flow without any white water. The lie I was interested in is about ten yards below the rough water, and about fifteen yards out from the bank. It is the ideal lie, which can be fished either up or downstream.

The rock which forms the lie is not large, but the accommodation must be comfortable. It is the preferred lie in this pool with every chance of a salmon resting in it—not asleep, I hoped.

When fished upstream, the salmon rises at the fly as it comes over the lie, and he takes in the manner of a large trout, rising slowly and majestically, intercepting the fly with effortless ease.

Fished downstream a salmon intent on the fly takes it when the fly has travelled about two feet past, taking it on the turn back into his lie. Occasionally a fish will follow the fly across the stream, and when the fly is stripped upstream, makes a darting slash at the fly without taking it. When a fish does slash at the fly he will take the fly within three or four more casts.

The wind was downstream and there was enough cockle on the water to hide me from the fish. The conditions were ideal for a downstream approach.

There was no need to crouch or crawl, just stand three yards back from the edge of the bank. The high bank on the other side shades the water and gives it a dark sheen which shows up the yellow of the fly and it is easily seen as is slips and slides across the ripple.

I greased the leader and the fly and the size 18 treble hook. The way the light wind was blowing, the cast was nearly square across and slightly downstream. I flicked a short line on to the water, fished it round, then lengthened line and cast again. These are the moments I enjoy. Each cast reaching out further and further towards the lie. The little Yellow Dolly floating with the current for a yard or two, and then sliding across the surface, bobbing over the waves as the line pulls it across the current. I like the anticipation of working down to a known lie, wondering whether he's there, whether he'll take. Nearer and nearer. Three more casts, two more, one, this time. The fly came across the lie, nothing, turned upstream, nothing. Another cast to the same spot, I gave it a little more time to float before moving it across the stream to come over the lie slightly lower downstream. Up came the fish, turned down with the fly. I lifted the rod, he was on. Hurrah, I had not lost my touch. Seventeen fish risen and untouched, the eighteenth was landed—a grilse of $5\frac{1}{2}$ lbs.

The problem was now squarely centred on the fly.

Unlike La Branche, who had fished his normal flies, I had used a different tying on a different hook to make my flies for the Canadian trip, and rather belatedly I was now convinced that the fly was at fault.

A comparison of the two flies showed they were similar in size and shape, and they both fished nicely on top of the water. This left only the hook as the prime problem area. The Yellow Dolly fished with the treble hook had the points protruding beyond the fringe of the skirt. Whereas the Canadian Dolly tied on a small single hook had the hook point shrouded by the skirt, also a treble hook has the points facing in three directions.

I do not accept Arthur Wood's theory of dislocated jaws, but it did have a similarity to my belief that summer fish mouth a fly very gently, and let it brush through their mouth. That's why when fishing with low water singles the salmon is hooked in the angle when allowed to turn down with the fly before tightening. Big springers in the cold waters of spring take hold of a fly like a terrier seizing a rat and the power of their jaws is such that they can crush the points of a size 4 treble 'till they nearly touch the shank. Possibly the sensitivity of the salmon increases as the temperature rises.

In Spring, numb with cold, the fish is very lethargic, fights deep and slow when hooked, and is easily tired out and appears not to feel pain as he crunches the fly. At the other end of the scale the Canadian fish in the higher water temperatures were very athletic, leaping out of the water many times, tireless in their fight and difficult to bring to the net and like my summer fish they did not chew the fly. All this left me with the feeling that the shrouding of the hook point was the reason for failing to hook the fish.

There is one little discrepancy, La Branche caught salmon in Canada on a large Palmer hackled fly, but could not do the same in Scotland. I catch them in Scotland on a tiny fly but could not use the same fly in Canada. Despite that I am certain a small Yellow Dolly will catch fish in Canada; they rose to the one I tied for the Canadian trip in the same manner as my fish even though I could not hook them.

I came back from Canada with the intention of experimenting with the Canadian dry flies and tying variants using their ideas. But after fishing with the single hook tying of the Yellow Dolly and discovering the reasons for failure time ran out on me. My river during 1985 had been in very good ply for fishing most of the very wet summer though I'm afraid it was a poor year for my style of fishing with all the spates. Every time the river fell to a nice level for dry fly it rained and ruined it. I gave up fishing at the start of the grouse shooting, the fish were too easy to catch with all the water about and the freezer was full.

*   *   *   *   *   *   *   *   *   *

The next year, 1986, the Spring was cold and the summer fishing did not start until the middle of June. The fish were held up for nearly a month by the low temperatures. When they did come up drought conditions followed very quickly and I was able to have a month fishing and experimenting in mainly low water conditions.

I spent a lot of time down the river as a ghillie for friends and experimenting with many dry fly variations.

The 'Bomber' I found to have no attraction for the salmon other than for one fish I tried it on who was rising at everything I put over him. It was quite amusing to see him come up alongside the orange hackled Bomber and give it a cold fishy stare and go down again. This fish also rose to a Rat Faced McDougall and followed a Buck Bug and a Yellow Dolly but he would not open his mouth for any of them.

I rose one fish on a Green Machine and touched another with it. I clicked two fish with little Buck Bugs one tied in green deer hair with an orange butt and one tied with Black Bear hair.

The only success I had with a Canadian fly was with a size 10 Butterfly which I greased, I found out later when reading the tying instructions that it is a wet fly!

I ghillied a friend down the river one beautiful sunny day. He caught two fish on some very old low water flies left to him by his father. The pattern was a Lady Caroline tied in true low water fashion with short bodies and very sparse wings. A No. 2 caught one at a water temperature of 56° and a No. 4 caught the other at a temperature of 60°. By three o'clock in the afternoon the water temperature had reached 66° with bright sunshine and not a cloud in the sky.

My friend fished the head of the Crooked Pool, wading in his bare feet the water was so warm. Nothing responded to his low water flies and when he gave up I tried a Bomber and a $\frac{3}{8}$" Yellow Dolly without any response. I put on the little Butterfly and I thought a fish moved to it as it came over the lie. It was such a vague flicker in the water that I couldn't be certain. I cast again and sure enough a fish came up and took it—a nice silver fish of 6 lbs.

We had a marvellous time fishing on a really lovely summer's day and to cap it all we watched a big dog otter hunting up the river then stalked him and took his photograph. He came out of the river at one point with an eel and ate it. When he finally spotted us he dived swam down the pool and sent a salmon hurtling out of the water.

Rob Wilson of Brora came up for a day's fishing. (Each year he takes the fishing for a week in July and brings his pals. The previous year when they had found the low water conditions frustrating and the fish impossible to catch, they asked Albert to instruct them in the art of dry fly fishing and they caught eight fish, firing Rob with an enthusiasm for Yellow Dollies).

We had never salmon fished together so I ghillied him down the river to show him the lies and the best way to fish the pools. He put up his 14 ft. rod at the first pool and selected a small Yellow Elver tube fly. I had taken the temperature which was 50° and suggested that his choice of pattern was fine but the size could be a wee bit bigger as the water was fairly cold. He changed to a fly tied on a $\frac{3}{4}''$ silver tube and as we set off for the pool I suggested like a good ghillie that we ought to go down the bank to the edge of the river and walk quietly downstream and stop some ten yards above the head of the pool out of sight of the fish. With his long rod he could easily cover the fish. At the second cast I saw a fish move to his fly. The next cast it took him and I left him to play and tail a 9 lb. fish while I took some photographs. He said that was the quickest he had ever caught a salmon.

Nothing more of interest happened until we got to the Rock Pool where a bonny grilse has alerted even though Rob was standing some six yards back from the bank and casting a fair line.

On to the next pool, where I suggested he put on a $\frac{1}{2}''$ tube of the same pattern as the temperature had risen. We crept down the edge of the water under the shelter of the bank again staying well back from the head of the pool. This time I set him a very tricky problem with lots of rocks jutting out of the water between him and the lie which was in between and just beyond the two farthest rocks.

I asked him to put the fly at his very first cast between and 2 yards beyond the two rocks. He did it with absolute perfection and the fish played his part by moving to the fly and then taking it on the next cast.

He fished a few more pools without any offers and then we turned for home. On the way back up the river I said I would fish a Yellow Dolly for the grilse in the Rock Pool to give him a practical demonstration of how I fish. We walked in a big half circle across the heather to be certain the fish didn't see us as I needed to be well upstream from the head of the pool. I crept down under the bank and Rob followed some 15 yards behind so that he could get a good view of everything I did. I fished down lengthening line and then crawled on for another eight yards to fish the middle lie. The grilse must have known that he was on stage. As the fly came over his lie he rose beautifully and turned down with the fly. Rob was absolutely thrilled. He had watched the whole proceedings and was fascinated by the way the little fly came across the water, as he said like a bumble bee, and then the thrill as the fish rose and took the fly down. He was kind enough to write later and say that he had learnt more that day than in many years of plodding away automatically casting and not really fishing. It came as a great surprise to him involved as he was with the better aspects of fishing to find that he had fallen into such a routine way of fishing.

I enjoyed all this concentrated fishing and watching the behaviour of the fish when confronted by the dozens of different creations I presented them with, Red Dollies, Green Dollies, Buck Bugs, Bombers and many others. I found out that the majority of Buck Bugs, Bombers and the Yellow Dollies tied on single hooks floated with the hook point parallel to the surface and not point down as I expected. I tied one fly on a Wilson low water size 12, using the sickly green deer hair spun and clipped to a cigar shape with three turns of brown hackle along its body. I gave it a yellow shawl-shaped tail and clipped the tail away from underneath the shank to clear the hook point. I hooked an eleven pound fish with it on 6 lb. nylon and landed it in spite of the point breaking off in its jaw. The same pattern hooked another which came off after about 4 mins and I also clicked two or three more. This pattern appears to have more potential than all the other flies I tried except the Yellow Dolly, and quite rightly is a hybrid cross between a Canadian 'Green Buck Bug' and a Yellow Dolly, so I called it 'Green Brolly'.

As my own river had been left undisturbed for two days I decided to put my Yellow Dollies to the test in the very low water without any wind to help me. I hooked and lost a fish which left me muttering away to myself as I wanted to catch a fish in what would be described by most fishermen as impossible conditions and I had muffed it.

However in the Stone Pool I hooked another fish which promptly put the line round a lump of sunken peat. A desperate throw of loose line freed it and I had him on the reel only for him to hang up again on the same lump of peat. This time he was fast and I could feel him bumping the line. In I jumped up to my arm pits but by the time I reached the line he was gone. I ducked under the water and retrieved my fly with two points straightened on the treble hook.

On the way home to get changed I felt the wind stir. My brothers and their friends were repairing the river side pony path as their way of making a contribution to the upkeep of the estate.

I stopped to chat and suggested they should knock off and go fishing because if the wind got a little stronger they would have a chance of a fish in the flat pools. They promptly downed tools got their rods and went in frantic haste down to the lower beat. I changed, went to the nearest flat pool and took two fish on the Yellow Dolly that I'd retrieved from the Stone Pool proving once again to my own satisfaction that fish can be caught in the lowest of water. My brothers and their friends underlined it by returning home with 4 more.

On the next day, the last day we were fishing before the July tenants took over on the Monday they all went down the river with a good strong wind blowing and putting a wave on the pools. None of them are experts but they are conditioned to the use of floating flies. I did not go down the river, I was too busy getting things ship shape for the fishing tenants. At supper that night I elicited from them that they had caught nine fish all from the still water pools fishing Yellow Dollies and small tube flies greased, stripping them over the waves. They said without being prompted that when the flies went under the water the fish would not come for them but when they were on the top the fish came many times and by clipping the flies smaller they made the fish take. One laddie said that a fish followed his fly nine times before it took him. He also added that if he had been fishing in a proper manner he would never have known that the fish was interested and he would have past it by!

Albert 'rang' me up at the end of the tenants first week to give me the news. There had been no rain and the river was very low and he had ghillied the tenant fisherman for five days. There had been some good windy days and they had caught 19 fish. I asked him how many they would have caught if he had not been looking after them? 'Two' he said without hesitation both caught on sub-surface flies. The other seventeen were caught on greased flies either dollies or small tubes after he had instructed each one in turn on concealment and the art of fishing a dry fly.

Heavy rains at the beginning of August ended six weeks of drought and brought to a close one of the best periods of low water fishing for quite a few years.

The river returned to its normal state of frequent spates followed by falling water. The fishing was excellent with many fish caught on normal sub-surface flies.

I continued my experiments which centred on white flies. I tied an all White Brolly fly on a No. 6 Captain Hamilton hook with a spun bear hair body and a nylon wool tail. The body I palmer hackled with an orange feather and fished with it on the slower dry fly pools. The water temperature had dropped to 54°, which is borderline for Yellow Dollies and I was curious to see if I could make a fish rise to a floating fly. The No. 6 White Brolly is slightly larger than my biggest Yellow Dolly and it fished quite nicely on top of the water in the slower pools. Success! I rose three fish on it and hooked one. This spurred me on to try other flies. The river yo-yo'd up and down with many spates followed by falling water, The water temperature fluctuated between 50° and 60°. Above 54° the fish would rise occasionally to the White Brolly without taking it and I used a Yellow Dolly or a Badger to catch them.

One afternoon I went down the river which had been falling for the past three days, the water temperature was 53° and I tried the White Brolly in the Pebble and Stone pools without moving a fish. These two pools are both ideal dry fly water with a bit of rough at the head followed by a smooth swift flow of deep water on a gentle curve with a gravel beach on the inside of the bend. It is very easy water to fish with a dry fly. The cast is made square across the pool and then left for the current to pull at the line and drag the fly across the main flow. As the fly comes out of the main current its movement is maintained by stripping line. Pondering what to try next I fiddled through my fly box with half a mind to revert to conventional flies. The Canadian Bomber took my eye. This had been a failure during the warm low water conditions of June and July. Far too big in my opinion for low water even though the guides in Canada said they used them when the water got very warm. Now I was faced with colder water and according to my theories I should use a larger fly. I picked the medium sized brown bodied Bomber with an orange body hackle and white head and tail tufts tied on the equivalent of a Partridge No. 2 nymph hook. I fished the Stone Pool down, round the bend and into the tail. I cast for the last cast and as the fly came round I started to strip. Suddenly without any warning a salmon hurled itself clear of the water in a dolphin like leap and took the Bomber as he dived back into the water. I was struck motionless. I have seen salmon and trout take a fly in that manner before but never in such a dramatic way. The fish leapt directly at me with torpedo like speed absolutely infuriated by the Orange-hackled Bomber. The whole moment was frozen into my mind and I was frozen to the spot. The moment passed, I lifted the rod and was firmly hooked into a grilse which I landed, tagged and returned to the river.

The river rose that night and it was two days before I could fish again. I was keen to turn my attention to Bombers to see if this spectacular performance had been a fluke. Here is a summary of the results.

I concentrated on the three sizes of Bombers that I had brought back from Canada. A very large one tied on a 2 inch long hook with a total length of $2\frac{3}{4}$ inches, brown deer hair body, brown body hackle and white head and tail tufts. The medium one I described and used in the Stone Pool and a small one tied in the same colours as the largest, on a hook similar to a No. 8 Partridge nymph hook. In addition to these Canadian flies I added a white head tuft to the White Brolly, to give me four sizes of Bombers to experiment with.

The lowest water temperature I fished was 50° and I had two of what the Canadians call 'hits' on the largest Bomber. 'Hits' is a very descriptive word for the way two quite large salmon struck the fly. Both fish hit the fly as they turned and I am quite certain they took it with their mouth but I did not hook either.

I did hook and land a fish at 50° on the medium size Bomber and this fly caught 5 fish at temperatures from 50° to 54° the variation in temperature was no doubt influenced by the height of water.

The smallest Bomber caught 4 fish at 54° and the white Bomber tied on the No. 6 Hamilton caught one in lowish water at 50°. The White Brolly without a head tuft caught one at 54° and one at the surprisingly high temperature of 60°. Nine fish were caught at temperatures from 50° to 54° on genuine Canadian Bombers during the first fortnight of August.

This performance by a Canadian dry fly pattern in Scotland should finally lay to rest the myth that salmon will not take a dry fly.

The Bomber with its head tuft and the longer body when tied on a long shank hook was by far the best of the Canadian flies at coping with rough water. Its 'floatability' is far superior to any of the other Canadian flies I tried and it stayed on the surface in rough water and rides the waves like a little long bodied duck with the white head tuft protruding like the short neck of a duck. Tied with an orange body hackle it shows up extremely well in the smaller sizes.

The method of fishing is definitely best when cast square across the rough water with the fly landing on the far side of the main current. The line bellies down stream with the current and then drags the fly along the side of the stream and then across. It takes very few casts to decide on the method of presentation which gives the best ride across the surface. The salmon certainly respond to this very curious fly and the response is to a fly scurrying across the current. I tried upstream presentation and floating the fly without drag but got no response. I must admit that I found the Bomber, contrary to all my previous feelings about it, to be a very exciting fly. I now have many ideas I want to try out in both colour and size.

I do not want to mislead you with my enthusiasm for the Bomber as a cold water fly (50° to 54°). If I had fished with conventional flies I think I would have caught more fish in the first few days following the spate. However there were two occasions in lowish water when the Bomber took fish after my conventional flies had failed. I shall certainly add it to my dry fly weaponry to extend my dry fly season.

What is very interesting about the Bomber is its similarity to a Col. Monell dry fly. The photograph I took shows the two flies have a similar bristly appearance and an overall size and bulk. The difference is in the body and this definitely confirms my feeling that the old idea about drag is due to the inability of a Palmer hackled fly to withstand immersion.

The Bomber and the Yellow Dolly when they get submerged by waves can be brought to the surface and remain floatable after many duckings. A conventionally tied dry fly, as the Col. Monell is, cannot withstand immersion and consequently upstream presentation must be the norm. The salmon in my opinion definitely prefer drag and that is why 'Dibbling' and the 'Hitch' used across the Atlantic and by some fishermen over here are very successful methods. The problem with all dry fly fishing is 'floatability'. Every effort must be made to keep the fly on top of the water. When a river is in spate the water races down and it is very difficult to get a conventional sub-surface fly to fish properly. The power of the current tends to hold a fly in the surface film and not wanting to bother with a sinking line in summer, I use brass bodied tubes. As the water falls so the speed of the current slackens and the change can be made to aluminium bodied tube flies or ordinary salmon flies. The moment comes in the falling water when a dry fly can be fished on some of the better dry fly pools without it being dragged under by swirling currents or drowned in rough water. Each day as the water falls away more water is available for the presentation of a dry fly and initially across and down is the better way to achieve the required drag on the fly. Then later, drag must be induced on the fly by stripping in the slower pools. The water continues to fall away to low water levels and then concealment becomes a problem and upstream presentation is necessary. This constant changing of the character of the river as the water falls away requires an intelligent approach to the many ways of presenting a fly. Rivers vary in the speed of run off and the rate at which they fall. I have said earlier that the third day after a spate on my river gives the best fishing. Other rivers will have a different timing but on any of them dry fly will be successful when the conditions are right.

I have fished many different rivers and I have only failed to catch salmon on a dry fly on two of them, one in Scotland and the other in Canada.

*   *   *   *   *   *   *   *   *

If you are still doubtful that salmon will take a floating fly then I will give you a little experiment to try.

When the water is warm and a good breeze ruffles the pool and you have moved a fish. Take one of your small tube flies, shorten the tube to a $\frac{1}{4}$ of an inch and clip the hair straight across to give an overall length of $\frac{1}{2}$ to $\frac{5}{8}$ of an inch.

Use a size 16 or 18 treble and grease the fly and the leader.

With care you should make the fly fish along the surface of the water. The results will surprise you, and you will reconsider everything I have said and understand why I take the trouble to tie a Yellow Dolly.

Of one thing I am certain, dry fly fishing will become an accepted way of catching salmon in Britain.

As I bring this book to an end there is one change I would like to see in the future and that is a more sporting attitude to fishing by fishermen adopting a personal limit to the number of fish they put in the bag.

There is great pleasure to be found in fishing and even more in the realisation that fish can be put back unharmed once personal needs are fulfilled. This is something that cannot be done in most field sports. It takes a deliberate decision to keep a fish.

In years to come 'Catch and Release' may well become the accepted norm in salmon fishing, and fishermen happy to accept a seasonal limit and yet able to enjoy unrestricted fishing by releasing the surplus.

I leave you to consider the future and what action you can take to save the Atlantic Salmon, and quote again the American's pleasure when he put back his first salmon.

'Gee! You should have seen him swim away.'

Index

References in italics are to book titles